Theodore Roosevelt

American Ideals

And Other Essays, Social and Political

By

Theodore Roosevelt

Author of "The Winning of the West," "The Wilderness
Hunter," "Hunting Trips of a Ranchman," etc.

With a Biographical Sketch by
Gen. Francis Vinton Greene

Patrick Henry University Press
Colorado Springs, Colorado

American Ideals and other Essays, Social and Political

by
Theodore Roosevelt

ISBN: 1-58963-321-0

Reprinted from the 1900 edition

Patrick Henry University Press
An Imprint of Fredonia Books
Colorado Springs, Colorado
http://www.patrickhenryuniversitypress.com

In order to make original editions of historical works available to scholars at an economical price, this facsimile of the original edition of 1900 is reproduced from the best available copy and has been digitally enhanced to improve legibility, but the text remains unaltered to retain historical authenticity.

BIOGRAPHICAL SKETCH

THE publishers of Theodore Roosevelt's books have decided to publish a popular edition of them during the Presidential campaign, and have asked me to write a few words of introduction. Few names are more widely known at the present moment than that of Theodore Roosevelt, so that in one sense any introduction is superfluous. But in this sense he is known chiefly as the " Rough Rider " of the Santiago campaign; whereas those who read these books will see that his experience as a volunteer officer in the war with Spain is only one incident in a life which has been singularly varied in thought and accomplishment and useful in many fields.

Roosevelt was born in New York City October 27, 1858. On his father's side he is descended from a Dutch emigrant of the seventeenth century, and the intermediate generations have been prudent, hard-working, successful merchants, prominent at all times in the commercial and social life of New York. His father's mother was from Pennsylvania, of Irish stock. His own mother was from Georgia, a daughter of James Dunwoodie Bullock, whose family was of Scotch and Huguenot origin, and had been prominent in public life in the South.

During his childhood, Roosevelt was in such bad health that it was doubtful if he would ever grow to manhood, and his robust strength and extraordinary capacity for physical endurance were not acquired until after his outdoor life in the West. He was educated at private schools in New York City, whence he went to Harvard University in 1876, graduating in the usual course in 1880. His tastes were for literary work, but the very year after leaving college he was elected to the Legislature as a representative of one of the City Assembly districts; and in the same fashion that has since characterized him, he plunged at once into the thick of

the fight as an ardent reformer, particularly
with reference to legislation affecting New
York City. His youth and lack of experience were more than counterbalanced by his
earnestness and aggressive energy, so that he
speedily became a power which had to be
recognized. He was the leader of his party
while it was in the minority, and when it was
in the majority he was Chairman of the Committee on Cities. He served three terms in
the Legislature, and during that time introduced and carried through more important
city legislation than was ever brought about
by any one assemblyman. It was all directed
by one central purpose, namely, to put an
end to boards and commissions with their
opportunities for " trades " and " deals," to
restrict the powers of the Board of Aldermen, who were notoriously corrupt, and to
concentrate responsibility in the Mayor and
single heads of departments, who could be
held accountable; in other words, to effect
the transformation from what was suitable for
town-meeting government in New England
or New Holland one or two centuries ago to

what was required for the complicated cosmopolitan metropolis of the nineteenth century.

While in the Legislature he still found time for literary work, and in 1882 wrote *The Naval War of 1812*, which told the story of our glorious successes on the sea; it was written at a period when our merchant marine was in decadence, our navy at its lowest ebb, and public interest in the subject almost wholly lost. It was not without its effect on the rebuilding of the navy which began two years later, which fortunately for us had already reached such a splendid development before 1898, and which is still in progress.

In 1884, severe domestic affliction and ill-health caused Roosevelt to abandon his work in New York and go to Wyoming. He invested a considerable part of what he inherited from his father in a cattle ranch, and intended and expected to remain in the West for many years. The wild, outdoor life fascinated him, and it brought him health and strength; in spite of defective eyesight he became a good shot, and was particularly fond of hunting big game — where the other

fellow had an even chance; and the peculiar
characteristics of the cowboy, since called
cow-puncher, appealed alike to his sense of
humor and his love of fair play. After he
returned to live in the East, his fondness for
hunting took him to the plains or mountains
for his vacation every year; and his hunting
experiences are charmingly described in two
volumes, *Hunting Trips of a Ranchman*
(1885) and *The Wilderness Hunter* (1893).
Senator Wolcott, in his speech notifying
Roosevelt of his nomination for the Vice-
Presidency, playfully referred to these hunting stories with the remark that " now that
you are our candidate they will all be believed "; but any one who enjoys or admires
manly sport — such as requires courage,
endurance, hardship, and a contest with
animals which are superior to man in
strength or speed—will take the stories on
faith, regardless of political belief.

Cattle raising did not prove financially
successful, though Roosevelt kept his ranch
until 1896. He returned to New York in
1886, married again, and once more plunged

into political life. A mayor of New York was to be elected that year. Abram S. Hewitt had received the nomination from Tammany Hall and other Democrats; Henry George was the candidate of the Socialists; the Republican party decided to put forward a candidate, and selected Roosevelt. There was but little chance of his election, but he made a most energetic canvass, speaking in three or four places every night during the latter part of the campaign. Hewitt was elected, George being second, and Roosevelt third with a vote of about 60,000 out of a total of 220,000.

The next three years were devoted almost wholly to literary and historical work. The upbuilding of the great West is one of the great world movements, in some respects the most important fact of the century now closing. Roosevelt began writing the story of it in 1886, under the title of *The Winning of the West ;* the first two volumes appearing in 1889, the third in 1894, and the fourth in 1896. Each volume describes a distinct period and is complete in itself. The last carried the story through the Louisiana Purchase. The history has been interrupted by the Spanish War and the engrossing duties of the office of Governor of New York; but it is hoped that the leisure hours of a Vice-President and the facilities of the libraries in Washington will afford the time and opportunity for its completion. Readers of the four volumes already published will understand the reasons why Roosevelt has such an extraordinary hold upon the sentiment and sympathy of the Western people. They will see that, although born and bred in the great city of the East, he realizes that the bone and sinew of this country, its strength and the sources of its wealth, are in the wide valley between the Alleghanies and the Rocky Mountains. Its origin and growth have been studied by him in every detail; he has participated enough in its life thoroughly to understand it, and he is in close touch and accord with its aspirations for the future.

In 1889, Roosevelt was appointed by President Harrison a member of the Civil Service Commission at Washington and soon became its president, retaining that office until the spring of 1895. A thorough believer in the principle of merit instead of favor in selecting and promoting appointees for the thousands of minor offices in the public service, he entered with his usual combativeness upon the task of enforcing the law for carrying this principle into effect. For six years, under his guidance, this was a fighting commission, not hesitating to grapple with any Cabinet officer or members of Congress, irrespective of their party affiliations, who tried to nullify or repeal the law. The result was the extension of the Civil Service rules to more than 50,000 government employés who were not protected by them in 1889.

In 1894 there was a union of all parties in New York City who were opposed to Tammany Hall, and W. L. Strong was elected Mayor. He invited Roosevelt to join his administration as head of one of the departments; first, as head of the Street-Cleaning Department, which he declined for lack of special knowledge; and second, as head of the Police Department, which he accepted.

Some of his friends in Washington urged him
not to accept the place on the ground that it
was beneath his dignity; others urged him
with even more vehemence to accept it, partly
because of the good work he could do for
New York in putting this department on an
honest basis, and partly because of the opportunity it would afford him of getting on the
firing-line in the contest for good government
in cities. He held this office for two years,
and though subjected to much criticism from
certain quarters for enforcing the liquor-
license law, yet it can be said, in a word, that
during his administration he placed the department on a thoroughly efficient basis,
broke up the organized system of blackmail
which had hitherto prevailed in the department, and gained the affectionate admiration
of the members of the force to an extent
which has never been equalled by any Police
Commissioner before or since.

During the three years from 1894 to 1897
he wrote the greater part of the essays on
political subjects which are printed in the
volumes of *American Ideals*.   In these will be

found his whole theory of politics, based on honesty, courage, never-ending hard work, and fair play; and coupled with these a certain measure of expediency which without sacrificing principle strives to get things done, and to accept the second best if what he considers the first best is not attainable; realizing that in a government of universal suffrage many minds must be consulted and a majority of them brought to the same conclusion before anything can be accomplished.

When President McKinley took office in 1897, he offered Roosevelt the position of Assistant Secretary of the Navy and it was promptly accepted.   He had been only a few months in office before he reached certain conclusions, to wit: that a war with Spain was inevitable, that it was desirable, and that he should take an active part in it.   He did everything that lay in his power during the nine months preceding April, 1898, to see that the Navy was prepared for the struggle, and how well he succeeded the officers of Dewey's and Sampson's fleets and the Bureau Chiefs in the Navy Department are always

abundantly able and willing to testify to. As
war drew near he began to make his plans for
his own part in it. He at first endeavored to
obtain a commission in one of the National
Guard regiments in New York which he felt
sure would volunteer for the war, but this
for various reasons being not practicable, he
determined to raise a regiment of volunteer
cavalry in the West. His friends in Washington did everything to dissuade him from
this project: his wife was ill, his little children were dependent on him, and it was
urged that he could render far more valuable
service in the Navy Department than in the
field. But his purpose was inflexible. On
account of his lack of experience in technical
military details he asked his friend, Dr.
Leonard Wood, an army surgeon who had
had much experience in Indian fighting in
Arizona, to take the position of Colonel, he
taking that of Lieutenant-Colonel. He persuaded the President to authorize the raising
of the 1st U. S. Volunteer Cavalry on this
basis. In about thirty days from the issuing
of this authority the regiment was recruited,

uniformed, drilled, armed, equipped, and transported to Tampa, Florida, ready for duty. The story of the Rough Riders is a household word from Maine to Arizona and from Oregon to Florida. As told by Roosevelt himself, it has been read by millions of readers. It is the most picturesque story in our military annals. In the first skirmish, after landing on Cuban soil, Wood was promoted to the rank of Brigadier-General, and Roosevelt was left in command of the regiment. It owed its origin to him, and he was associated with it from start to finish.

In September, 1898, the Republican State Convention met to nominate a candidate for Governor of New York. Roosevelt was then with his regiment at Montauk Point, about to be mustered out of service. He was nominated, and at once entered upon a vigorous campaign. The party was then suffering from criticism on account of its alleged mismanagement of the canals, and in the opinion of the best judges any other candidate would have been defeated. Roosevelt was elected by about 20,000 majority.

His election was doubtless due to his services in the war with Spain, but these contributed little or nothing to his qualifications for the office. These were found in his experience in the State Legislature, in the Civil Service Commission, the Police Department, and the Navy Department, an experience which had given him an intimate knowledge of the practical working of municipal, state, and national governments; and above all, to his fearless honesty and tireless energy in devotion to sound principles of administration. During his two years of office, as Governor, he has set a standard which the people of New York will not soon allow to be lowered. He has put through a first-class Civil Service law, he has framed and carried through legislation in regard to the difficult question of taxation, based on a new principle which is perfectly equitable, is particularly suited to modern conditions, and when modified in details to such extent as experience shall demonstrate to be necessary will be accepted by all; he has honestly and economically administered the canals, and has caused the canal question to be carefully studied so as to bring out all the essential facts upon which its solution must be based; he has resolutely refused to appoint any unfit man to office, although usually ready to accept a suitable man when recommended by the Republican organization, which includes the greater part of the voters in the party; he has appointed commissions to study the educational system, the tenement-house question, and a revision of the Charter of the great city of New York. His appointees, from top to bottom, have been of the very highest type; from the foundation of the State there have been no higher.

Many of his measures are in a half-finished condition. The Republicans of New York would, beyond question, have renominated and re-elected him to carry them to completion. But at this stage the Republicans of the United States with singular unanimity have called him away from New York, against his personal wishes and judgment, to take part in national affairs and to aid President McKinley in carrying out those policies which during the last four years have brought such prosperity at home and such greatness abroad. He has yielded his judgment to theirs, and cheerfully accepted the call.

He has six children—Alice Lee, Theodore, Kermit, Ethel Carow, Archibald Bullock, and Quentin. His home is at Sagamore Hill, Oyster Bay, Long Island.

In these pages the people of this land can read the thoughts that have been spun out by his brain during the last eighteen years, and can see what manner of man he is. They believe him to be honest, fearless, straightforward, a tireless worker, experienced in the administration of city, state, and national affairs, a careful student and writer of his country's history, an American in every fibre, a man who holds his life at his country's service whenever a war is on during his lifetime. In reading these books their belief in him will be justified and confirmed.

FRANCIS V. GREENE.

NEW YORK, July 16, 1900.

PREFACE

IT is not difficult to be virtuous in a cloistered and negative way. Neither is it
difficult to succeed, after a fashion, in active
life, if one is content to disregard the considerations which bind honorable and upright men. But it is by no means easy to
combine honesty and efficiency; and yet it is
absolutely necessary, in order to do any work
really worth doing. It is not hard, while
sitting in one's study, to devise admirable
plans for the betterment of politics and of
social conditions; but in practice it too often
proves very hard to make any such plan
work at all, no matter how imperfectly.
Yet the effort must continually be made,
under penalty of constant retrogression in
our political life.

No one quality or one virtue is enough to

insure success; vigor, honesty, common sense,—all are needed. The practical man is merely rendered more noxious by his practical ability if he employs it wrongly, whether from ignorance or from lack of morality; while the doctrinaire, the man of theories, whether written or spoken, is useless if he cannot also act.

These essays are written on behalf of the many men who do take an actual part in trying practically to bring about the conditions for which we somewhat vaguely hope; on behalf of the under-officers in that army which, with much stumbling, halting, and slipping, many mistakes and shortcomings, and many painful failures, does, nevertheless, through weary strife, accomplish something toward raising the standard of public life.

We feel that the doer is better than the critic and that the man who strives stands far above the man who stands aloof, whether he thus stands aloof because of pessimism or because of sheer weakness. To borrow a simile from the football field, we believe that men must play fair, but that there must be no shirking, and that success can only come to the player who " hits the line hard."

THEODORE ROOSEVELT.

SAGAMORE HILL,
    October, 1897.

CONTENTS

CONTENTS

I

AMERICAN IDEALS[1]

IN his noteworthy book on *National Life and Character*, Mr. Pearson says: "The countrymen of Chatham and Wellington, of Washington and Lincoln, in short the citizens of every historic state, are richer by great deeds that have formed the national character, by winged words that have passed into current speech, by the examples of lives and labors consecrated to the service of the commonwealth." In other words, every great nation owes to the men whose lives have formed part of its greatness not merely the material effect of what they did, not merely the laws they placed upon the statute books or the victories they won over armed foes, but also the immense but indefinable

[1] *The Forum*, February, 1895.

25

moral influence produced by their deeds and
words themselves upon the national character. It would be difficult to exaggerate the
material effects of the careers of Washington
and of Lincoln upon the United States.
Without Washington we should probably
never have won our independence of the
British crown, and we should almost certainly have failed to become a great nation,
remaining instead a cluster of jangling little
communities, drifting toward the type of
government prevalent in Spanish America.
Without Lincoln we might perhaps have
failed to keep the political unity we had won;
and even if, as is possible, we had kept it,
both the struggle by which it was kept and
the results of this struggle would have been
so different that the effect upon our national
history could not have failed to be profound. Yet the nation's debt to these men is
not confined to what it owes them for its
material well-being, incalculable though this
debt is.   Beyond the fact that we are an
independent and united people, with half a

continent as our heritage, lies the fact that every American is richer by the heritage of the noble deeds and noble words of Washington and of Lincoln. Each of us who reads the Gettysburg speech or the second inaugural address of the greatest American of the nineteenth century, or who studies the long campaigns and lofty statesmanship of that other American who was even greater, cannot but feel within him that lift toward things higher and nobler which can never be bestowed by the enjoyment of mere material prosperity.

It is not only the country which these men helped to make and helped to save that is ours by inheritance; we inherit also all that is best and highest in their characters and in their lives. We inherit from Lincoln and from the might of Lincoln's generation not merely the freedom of those who once were slaves; for we inherit also the fact of the freeing of them, we inherit the glory and the honor and the wonder of the deed that was done, no less than the actual results of the deed when done. The bells that rang at the passage of the Emancipation Proclamation still ring in Whittier's ode; and as men think over the real nature of the triumph then scored for humankind their hearts shall ever throb as they cannot over the greatest industrial success or over any victory won at a less cost than ours.

The captains and the armies who, after long years of dreary campaigning and bloody, stubborn fighting, brought to a close the Civil War have likewise left us even more than a reunited realm. The material effect of what they did is shown in the fact that the same flag flies from the Great Lakes to the Rio Grande, and all the people of the United States are richer because they are one people and not many, because they belong to one great nation and not to a contemptible knot of struggling nationalities. But besides this, besides the material results of the Civil War, we are all, North and South, incalculably richer for its memories.

We are the richer for each grim campaign, for each hard-fought battle. We are the richer for valor displayed alike by those who fought so valiantly for the right and by those who, no less valiantly, fought for what they deemed the right. We have in us nobler capacities for what is great and good because of the infinite woe and suffering, and because of the splendid ultimate triumph.

In the same way that we are the better for the deeds of our mighty men who have served the nation well, so we are the worse for the deeds and the words of those who have striven to bring evil on the land. Most fortunately we have been free from the peril of the most dangerous of all examples. We have not had to fight the influence exerted over the minds of eager and ambitious men by the career of the military adventurer who heads some successful revolutionary or separatist movement. No man works such incalculable woe to a free country as he who teaches young men that one of the paths to glory, renown, and temporal success lies along the line of armed resistance to the Government, of its attempted overthrow.

Yet if we are free from the peril of this example, there are other perils from which we are not free. All through our career we have had to war against a tendency to regard, in the individual and the nation alike, as most important, things that are of comparatively little importance. We rightfully value success, but sometimes we overvalue it, for we tend to forget that success may be obtained by means which should make it abhorred and despised by every honorable man. One section of the community deifies as "smartness" the kind of trickery which enables a man without conscience to succeed in the financial or political world. Another section of the community deifies violent homicidal lawlessness. If ever our people as a who'e adopt these views, then we shall have proved that we are unworthy of the heritage our forefathers left us; and our country will go down in ruin.

The people that do harm in the end are not the wrong-doers whom all execrate; they are the men who do not do quite as much wrong, but who are applauded instead of being execrated. The career of Benedict Arnold has done us no harm as a nation because of the universal horror it inspired. The men who have done us harm are those who have advocated disunion, but have done it so that they have been enabled to keep their political position; who have advocated repudiation of debts, or other financial dishonesty, but have kept their standing in the community; who preach the doctrines of anarchy, but refrain from action that will bring them within the pale of the law; for these men lead thousands astray by the fact that they go unpunished or even rewarded for their misdeeds.

It is unhappily true that we inherit the evil as well as the good done by those who have gone before us, and in the one case as in the other the influence extends far beyond the mere material effects. The foes of order harm quite as much by example as by what they actually accomplish. So it is with the equally dangerous criminals of the wealthy classes. The conscienceless stock speculator who acquires wealth by swindling his fellows, by debauching judges and corrupting legislatures, and who ends his days with the reputation of being among the richest men in America, exerts over the minds of the rising generation an influence worse than that of the average murderer or bandit, because his career is even more dazzling in its success, and even more dangerous in its effects upon the community. Any one who reads the essays of Charles Francis Adams and Henry Adams, entitled " A Chapter of Erie," and " The Gold Conspiracy in New York,"will read about the doings of men whose influence for evil upon the community is more potent than that of any band of anarchists or train robbers.

There are other members of our mercantile community who, being perfectly honest themselves, nevertheless do almost as much damage as the dishonest. The profesional labor agitator, with all his reckless incendiarism of speech, can do no more harm than the narrow, hard, selfish merchant or manufacturer who deliberately sets himself to keep the laborers he employs in a condition of dependence which will render them helpless to combine against him; and every such merchant or manufacturer who rises to sufficient eminence leaves the record of his name and deeds as a legacy of evil to all who come after him.

But of course the worst foes of America are the foes to that orderly liberty without which our Republic must speedily perish. The reckless labor agitator who arouses the mob to riot and bloodshed is in the last analysis the most dangerous of the workingman's enemies. This man is a real peril; and so is his sympathizer, the legislator, who to catch votes denounces the judiciary and the military because they put down mobs. We Americans have, on the whole, a right to be optimists; but it is mere folly to blind

ourselves to the fact that there are some
black clouds on the horizon of our future.

During the summer of 1894, every American capable of thinking must at times have
pondered very gravely over certain features
of the national character which were brought
into unpleasant prominence by the course of
events. The demagogue, in all his forms, is
as characteristic an evil of a free society as
the courtier is of a despotism; and the attitude of many of our public men at the
time of the great strike in July, 1894, was
such as to call down on their heads the hearty
condemnation of every American who
wishes well to his country. It would be
difficult to overestimate the damage done by
the example and action of a man like Governor Altgeld of Illinois. Whether he is
honest or not in his beliefs is not of the
slightest consequence. He is as emphatically
the foe of decent government as Tweed
himself, and is capable of doing far more
damage than Tweed. The Governor, who
began his career by pardoning anarchists,

and whose most noteworthy feat since was his bitter and undignified, but fortunately futile, campaign against the election of the upright judge who sentenced the anarchists, is the foe of every true American and is the foe particularly of every honest working-man. With such a man it was to be expected that he should in time of civic commotion act as the foe of the law-abiding and the friend of the lawless classes, and endeavor, in company with the lowest and most abandoned office-seeking politicians, to prevent proper measures being taken to prevent riot and to punish the rioters. Had it not been for the admirable action of the Federal Government, Chicago would have seen a repetition of what occurred during the Paris Commune, while Illinois would have been torn by a fierce social war; and for all the horrible waste of life that this would have entailed Governor Altgeld would have been primarily responsible. It was a most fortunate thing that the action at Washington was so quick and so emphatic.

Senator Davis of Minnesota set the key of patriotism at the time when men were still puzzled and hesitated. The President and Attorney-General Olney acted with equal wisdom and courage, and the danger was averted. The completeness of the victory of the Federal authorities, representing the cause of law and order, has been perhaps one reason why it was so soon forgotten; and now not a few shortsighted people need to be reminded that when we were on the brink of an almost terrific explosion the governor of Illinois did his best to work to this country a measure of harm as great as any ever planned by Benedict Arnold, and that we were saved by the resolute action of the Federal judiciary and of the regular army. Moreover, Governor Altgeld, though preeminent, did not stand alone on his unenviable prominence. Governor Waite of Colorado stood with him. Most of the Populist governors of the Western States, and the Republican governor of California and the Democratic governor of North Dakota, shared the shame with him; and it makes no difference whether in catering to riotous mobs they paid heed to their own timidity and weakness, or to that spirit of blatant demagogism which, more than any other, jeopardizes the existence of free institutions. On the other hand, the action of the then Governor of Ohio, Mr. McKinley, entitled him to the gratitude of all good citizens.

Every true American, every man who thinks, and who if the occasion comes is ready to act, may do well to ponder upon the evil wrought by the lawlessness of the disorderly classes when once they are able to elect their own chiefs to power. If the Government generally got into the hands of men such as Altgeld, the Republic would go to pieces in a year; and it would be right that it should go to pieces, for the election of such men shows that the people electing them are unfit to be entrusted with self-government.

There are, however, plenty of wrongdoers besides those who commit the overt act. Too much cannot be said against the

men of wealth who sacrifice everything to
getting wealth. There is not in the world
a more ignoble character than the mere
money-getting American, insensible to every
duty, regardless of every principle, bent only
on amassing a fortune, and putting his fortune only to the basest uses—whether these
uses be to speculate in stocks and wreck
railroads himself, or to allow his son to lead
a life of foolish and expensive idleness and
gross debauchery, or to purchase some scoundrel of high social position, foreign or native,
for his daughter. Such a man is only the
more dangerous if he occasionally does some
deed like founding a college or endowing a
church, which makes those good people who
are also foolish forget his real iniquity.
These men are equally careless of the workingmen, whom they oppress, and of the state,
whose existence they imperil. There are not
very many of them, but there is a very great
number of men who approach more or less
closely to the type, and, just in so far as
they do so approach, they are curses to the

country. The man who is content to let politics go from bad to worse, jesting at the curruption of politicians, the man who is content to see the maladministration of justice without an immediate and resolute effort to reform it, is shirking his duty and is preparing the way for infinite woe in the future. Hard, brutal indifference to the right, and an equally brutal shortsightedness as to the inevitable results of corruption and injustice, are baleful beyond measure; and yet they are characteristic of a great many Americans who think themselves perfectly respectable, and who are considered thriving, prosperous men by their easy-going fellow-citizens.

Another class, merging into this, and only less dangerous, is that of the men whose ideals are purely material. These are the men who are willing to go for good government when they think it will pay, but who measure everything by the shop-till, the people who are unable to appreciate any quality that is not a mercantile commodity, who do not under-

stand that a poet may do far more for a
country than the owner of a nail factory,
who do not realize that no amount of commercial prosperity can supply the lack of the
heroic virtues, or can in itself solve the terrible social problems which all the civilized
world is now facing. The mere materialist
is, above all things, shortsighted. In a recent article Mr. Edward Atkinson casually
mentioned that the regular army could now
render the country no " effective or useful
service." Two months before this sapient
remark was printed the regular army had
saved Chicago from the fate of Paris in
1870 and had prevented a terrible social war
in the West. At the end of this article Mr.
Atkinson indulged in a curious rhapsody
against the navy, denouncing its existence
and being especially wrought up, not because war-vessels take life, but because they
" destroy commerce." To men of a certain kind, trade and property are far more
sacred than life or honor, of far more con-

sequence than the great thoughts and lofty emotions, which alone make a nation mighty. They believe, with a faith almost touching in its utter feebleness, that "the Angel of Peace, draped in a garment of untaxed calico," has given her final message to men when she has implored them to devote all their energies to producing oleomargarine at a quarter of a cent less a firkin, or to importing woollens for a fraction less than they can be made at home. These solemn prattlers strive after an ideal in which they shall happily unite the imagination of a green-grocer with the heart of a Bengalee baboo. They are utterly incapable of feeling one thrill of generous emotion, or the slightest throb of that pulse which gives to the world statesmen, patriots, warriors, and poets, and which makes a nation other than a cumberer of the world's surface. In the concluding page of his article Mr. Atkinson, complacently advancing his panacea, his quack cure-all, says that " all evil powers of

the world will go down before " a policy of
" reciprocity of trade without obstruction "!
Fatuity can go no farther.

No Populist who wishes a currency based
on corn and cotton stands in more urgent
need of applied common sense than does the
man who believes that the adoption of any
policy, no matter what, in reference to our
foreign commerce, will cut that tangled knot
of social well-being and misery at which the
fingers of the London free-trader clutch as
helplessly as those of the Berlin protection-
ist. Such a man represents individually an
almost imponderable element in the work
and thought of the community; but in the
aggregate he stands for a real danger, because he stands for a feeling evident of late
years among many respectable people. The
people who pride themselves upon having a
purely commercial ideal are apparently unaware that such an ideal is as essentially mean
and sordid as any in the world, and that no
bandit community of the Middle Ages can
have led a more unlovely life than would

be the life of men to whom trade and man-
ufactures were everything, and to whom
such words as national honor and glory, as
courage and daring, and loyalty and unself-
ishness, had become meaningless. The merely
material, the merely commercial ideal, the
ideal of the men " whose fatherland is the
till," is in its very essence debasing and low-
ering. It is as true now as ever it was that
no man and no nation shall live by bread
alone. Thrift and industry are indispensable
virtues; but they are not all-sufficient. We
must base our appeals for civic and national
betterment on nobler grounds than those of
mere business expediency.

We have examples enough and to spare
that tend to evil; nevertheless, for our good
fortune, the men who have most impressed
themselves upon the thought of the nation
have left behind them careers the influence
of which must tell for good. The unscrupulous speculator who rises to enormous
wealth by swindling his neighbor; the capitalist who oppresses the workingman; the

agitator who wrongs the workingman yet more deeply by trying to teach him to rely not upon himself, but partly upon the charity of individuals or of the state and partly upon mob violence; the man in public life who is a demagogue or corrupt, and the newspaper writer who fails to attack him because of his corruption, or who slanderously assails him when he is honest; the political leader who, cursed by some obliquity of moral or of mental vision, seeks to produce sectional or social strife—all these, though important in their day, have hitherto failed to leave any lasting impress upon the life of the nation, The men who have profoundly influenced the growth of our national character have been in most cases precisely those men whose influence was for the best and was strongly felt as antagonistic to the worst tendency of the age. The great writers, who have written in prose or verse, have done much for us. The great orators whose burning words on behalf of liberty, of union, of honest government, have rung through our legislative halls, have done even more. Most of all has been done by the men who have spoken to us through deeds and not words, or whose words have gathered their especial charm and significance because they came from men who did speak in deeds. A nation's greatness lies in its possibility of achievement in the present, and nothing helps it more than the consciousness of achievement in the past.

II

TRUE AMERICANISM [1]

PATRIOTISM was once defined as "the last refuge of a scoundrel"; and somebody has recently remarked that when Dr. Johnson gave this definition he was ignorant of the infinite possibilities contained in the word " reform." Of course both gibes were quite justifiable, in so far as they were aimed at people who use noble names to cloak base purposes. Equally of course the man shows little wisdom and a low sense of duty who fails to see that love of country is one of the elemental virtues, even though scoundrels play upon it for their own selfish ends; and, inasmuch as abuses continually grow up in civic life as in all other kinds of life, the statesman is indeed a weakling who

[1] *The Forum*, April, 1894.

hesitates to reform these abuses because the word " reform " is often on the lips of men who are silly or dishonest.

What is true of patriotism and reform is true also of Americanism. There are plenty of scoundrels always ready to try to belittle reform movements or to bolster up existing iniquities in the name of Americanism; but this does not alter the fact that the man who can do most in this country is and must be the man whose Americanism is most sincere and intense. Outrageous though it is to use a noble idea as the cloak for evil, it is still worse to assail the noble idea itself because it can thus be used. The men who do iniquity in the name of patriotism, of reform, of Americanism, are merely one small division of the class that has always existed and will always exist,—the class of hypocrites and demagogues, the class that is always prompt to steal the watchwords of righteousness and use them in the interests of evil-doing.

The stoutest and truest Americans are the

very men who have the least sympathy with the people who invoke the spirit of Americanism to aid what is vicious in our government or to throw obstacles in the way of those who strive to reform it. It is contemptible to oppose a movement for good because that movement has already succeeded somewhere else, or to champion an existing abuse because our people have always been wedded to it. To appeal to national prejudice against a given reform movement is in every way unworthy and silly. It is as childish to denounce free trade because England has adopted it as to advocate it for the same reason. It is eminently proper, in dealing with the tariff, to consider the effect of tariff legislation in time past upon other nations as well as the effect upon our own; but in drawing conclusions it is in the last degree foolish to try to excite prejudice against one system because it is in vogue in some given country, or to try to excite prejudice in its favor because the economists of that country have found that it was suited to their own peculiar needs. In attempting to solve our difficult problem of municipal government it is mere folly to refuse to profit by whatever is good in the examples of Manchester and Berlin because these cities are foreign, exactly as it is mere folly blindly to copy their examples without reference to our own totally different conditions. As for the absurdity of declaiming against civil-service reform, for instance, as " Chinese," because written examinations have been used in China, it would be quite as wise to declaim against gunpowder because it was first utilized by the same people. In short, the man who, whether from mere dull fatuity or from an active interest in misgovernment, tries to appeal to American prejudice against things foreign, so as to induce Americans to oppose any measure for good, should be looked on by his fellow-countrymen with the heartiest contempt. So much for the men who appeal to the spirit of Americanism to sustain us in wrong-doing. But we must never let our contempt for these men blind us to the nobility of the idea which they strive to degrade.

We Americans have many grave problems to solve, many threatening evils to fight, and many deeds to do, if, as we hope and believe, we have the wisdom, the strength, the courage, and the virtue to do them. But we must face facts as they are. We must neither surrender ourselves to a foolish optimism, nor succumb to a timid and ignoble pessimism. Our nation is that one among all the nations of the earth which holds in its hands the fate of the coming years. We enjoy exceptional advantages, and are menaced by exceptional dangers; and all signs indicate that we shall either fail greatly or succeed greatly. I firmly believe that we shall succeed; but we must not foolishly blink the dangers by which we are threatened, for that is the way to fail. On the contrary, we must soberly set to work to find out all we can about the existence and extent of every evil, must acknowledge it to be such, and must then attack it with unyield-

ing resolution. There are many such evils,
and each must be fought after a separate
fashion; yet there is one quality which we
must bring to the solution of every problem,—that is, an intense and fervid Americanism. We shall never be successful over
the dangers that confront us; we shall never
achieve true greatness, nor reach the lofty
ideal which the founders and preservers of
our mighty Federal Republic have set before
us, unless we are Americans in heart and
soul, in spirit and purpose, keenly alive to
the responsibility implied in the very name
of American, and proud beyond measure of
the glorious privilege of bearing it.

There are two or three sides to the question of Americanism, and two or three senses
in which the word "Americanism" can be
used to express the antithesis of what is unwholesome and undesirable. In the first
place we wish to be broadly American and
national, as opposed to being local or sectional. We do not wish, in politics, in literature, or in art, to develop that unwholesome

parochial spirit, that over-exaltation of the little community at the expense of the great nation, which produces what has been described as the patriotism of the village, the patriotism of the belfry. Politically, the indulgence of this spirit was the chief cause of the calamities which befell the ancient republics of Greece, the mediæval republics of Italy, and the petty States of Germany as it was in the last century. It is this spirit of provincial patriotism, this inability to take a view of broad adhesion to the whole nation that has been the chief among the causes that have produced such anarchy in the South American States, and which have resulted in presenting to us, not one great Spanish-American federal nation stretching from the Rio Grande to Cape Horn, but a squabbling multitude of revolution-ridden States, not one of which stands even in the second rank as a power. However, politically this question of American nationality has been settled once for all. We are no longer in danger of repeating in our history the shameful and contemptible disasters that have befallen the Spanish possessions on this continent since they threw off the yoke of Spain. Indeed there is, all through our life, very much less of this parochial spirit than there was formerly. Still there is an occasional outcropping here and there; and it is just as well that we should keep steadily in mind the futility of talking of a Northern literature or a Southern literature, an Eastern or a Western school of art or science. Joel Chandler Harris is emphatically a national writer; so is Mark Twain. They do not write merely for Georgia or Missouri or California any more than for Illinois or Connecticut; they write as Americans and for all people who can read English. St. Gaudens lives in New York; but his work is just as distinctive of Boston or Chicago. It is of very great consequence that we should have a full and ripe literary development in the United States, but it is not of the least consequence whether New York, or Boston, or Chicago, or San Francisco becomes the literary or artistic centre of the United States.

There is a second side to this question of a broad Americanism, however. The patriotism of the village or the belfry is bad, but the lack of all patriotism is even worse. There are philosophers who assure us, that in the future, patriotism will be regarded not as a virtue at all, but merely as a mental stage in the journey toward a state of feeling when our patriotism will include the whole human race and all the world. This may be so; but the age of which these philosophers speak is still several aeons distant. In fact, philosophers of this type are so very advanced that they are of no practical service to the present generation. It may be, that in ages so remote that we cannot now understand any of the feelings of those who will dwell in them, patriotism will no longer be regarded as a virtue, exactly as it may be that in those remote ages people will look down upon and disregard monogamic marriage; but as things now are and have been for two or three thousand years past, and are likely to be for two or three thousand years to come, the words "home" and "country" mean a great deal. Nor do they show any tendency to lose their significance. At present, treason, like adultery, ranks as one of the worst of all possible crimes.

One may fall very far short of treason and yet be an undesirable citizen in the community. The man who becomes Europeanized, who loses his power of doing good work on this side of the water, and who loses his love for his native land, is not a traitor; but he is a silly and undesirable citizen. He is as emphatically a noxious element in our body politic as is the man who comes here from abroad and remains a foreigner. Nothing will more quickly or more surely disqualify a man from doing good work in the world than the acquirement of that flaccid habit of mind which its possessors style cosmopolitanism.

It is not only necessary to Americanize the immigrants of foreign birth who settle

among us, but it is even more necessary for
those among us who are by birth and descent already Americans not to throw away
our birthright, and, with incredible and contemptible folly, wander back to bow down
before the alien gods whom our forefathers
forsook. It is hard to believe that there is
any necessity to warn Americans that, when
they seek to model themselves on the lines of
other civilizations, they make themselves the
butts of all right-thinking men; and yet the
necessity certainly exists to give this warning to many of our citizens who pride themselves on their standing in the world of art
and letters, or, perchance, on what they
would style their social leadership in the community. It is always better to be an original than an imitation, even when the imitation is of something better than the original; but what shall we say of the fool who is
content to be an imitation of something
worse? Even if the weaklings who seek to
be other than Americans were right in deem-
ing other nations to be better than their own,

the fact yet remains that to be a first-class American is fifty-fold better than to be a second-class imitation of a Frenchman or Englishman. As a matter of fact, however, those of our countrymen who do believe in American inferiority are always individuals who, however cultivated, have some organic weakness in their moral or mental make-up; and the great mass of our people, who are robustly patriotic, and who have sound, healthy minds, are justified in regarding these feeble renegades with a half-impatient and half-amused scorn.

We believe in waging relentless war on rank-growing evils of all kinds, and it makes no difference to us if they happen to be of purely native growth. We grasp at any good, no matter whence it comes. We do not accept the evil attendant upon another system of government as an adequate excuse for that attendant upon our own; the fact that the courtier is a scamp does not render the demagogue any the less a scoundrel. But it remains true that, in spite of all our

faults and shortcomings, no other land offers such glorious possibilities to the man
able to take advantage of them, as does ours;
it remains true that no one of our people can
do any work really worth doing unless he does
it primarily as an American. It is because
certain classes of our people still retain their
spirit of colonial dependence on, and exag-
gerated deference to, European opinion, that
they fail to accomplish what they ought to.
It is precisely along the lines where we have
worked most independently that we have accomplished the greatest results; and it is in
those professions where there has been no
servility to, but merely a wise profiting by,
foreign experience, that we have produced
our greatest men. Our soldiers and statesmen and orators; our explorers, our wilder-
ness-winners, and commonwealth-builders;
the men who have made our laws and seen
that they were executed; and the other men
whose energy and ingenuity have created
our marvellous material prosperity,—all
these have been men who have drawn wis-

dom from the experience of every age and nation, but who have nevertheless thought, and worked, and conquered, and lived. and died, purely as Americans; and on the whole they have done better work than has been done in any other country during the short period of our national life.

On the other hand, it is in those professions where our people have striven hardest to mould themselves in conventional European forms that they have succeeded least; and this holds true to the present day, the failure being of course most conspicuous where the man takes up his abode in Europe; where he becomes a second-rate European, because he is over-civilized, over-sensitive, over-refined, and has lost the hardihood and manly courage by which alone he can conquer in the keen struggle of our national life. Be it remembered, too, that this same being does not really become a European; he only ceases being an American, and becomes nothing. He throws away a great prize for the sake of a lesser one, and does not even get the lesser one. The painter who goes to Paris, not merely to get two or three years' thorough training in his art, but with the deliberate purpose of taking up his abode there, and with the intention of following in the ruts worn deep by ten thousand earlier travellers, instead of striking off to rise or fall on a new line, thereby forfeits all chance of doing the best work. He must content himself with aiming at that kind of mediocrity which consists in doing fairly well what has already been done better; and he usually never even sees the grandeur and picturesqueness lying open before the eyes of every man who can read the book of America's past and the book of America's present. Thus it is with the undersized man of letters, who flees his country because he, with his delicate, effeminate sensitiveness, finds the conditions of life on this side of the water crude and raw; in other words, because he finds that he cannot play a man's part among men, and so goes where he will be sheltered from the winds that harden stouter souls. This *emigré* may write graceful and pretty verses, essays, novels; but he will never do work to compare with that of his brother, who is strong enough to stand on his own feet, and do his work as an American. Thus it is with the scientist who spends his youth in a German university, and can thenceforth work only in the fields already fifty times furrowed by the German ploughs. Thus it is with that most foolish of parents who sends his children to be educated abroad, not knowing— what every clear-sighted man from Washington and Jay down has known—that the American who is to make his way in America should be brought up among his fellow Americans. It is among the people who like to consider themselves, and, indeed, to a large extent are, the leaders of the so-called social world, especially in some of the north-eastern cities, that this colonial habit of thought, this thoroughly provincial spirit of admiration for things foreign, and inability to stand on one's own feet, becomes most evident and most despicable. We believe in every kind of honest and lawful pleasure, so long as the getting it is not made man's chief business; and we believe heartily in the good that can be done by men of leisure who work hard in their leisure, whether at politics or philanthropy, literature or art. But a leisure class whose leisure simply means idleness is a curse to the community, and in so far as its members distinguish themselves chiefly by aping the worst—not the best—traits of similar people across the water, they become both comic and noxious elements of the body politic.

The third sense in which the word "Americanism" may be employed is with reference to the Americanizing of the newcomers to our shores. We must Americanize them in every way, in speech, in political ideas and principles, and in their way of looking at the relations between Church and State. We welcome the German or the Irishman who becomes an American. We have no use for the German or Irishman who remains such.

We do not wish German-Americans and Irish-Americans who figure as such in our social and political life; we want only Americans, and, provided they are such, we do not care whether they are of native or of Irish or of German ancestry. We have no room in any healthy American community for a German-American vote or an Irish-American vote, and it is contemptible demagogy to put planks into any party platform with the purpose of catching such a vote. We have no room for any people who do not act and vote simply as Americans, and as nothing else. Moreover, we have as little use for people who carry religious prejudices into our politics as for those who carry prejudices of caste or nationality. We stand unalterably in favor of the public-school system in its entirety. We believe that English and no other language, is that in which all the school exercises should be conducted. We are against any division of the school fund, and against any appropriation of public money for sectarian purposes. We are

against any recognition whatever by the
State in any shape or form of State-aided
parochial schools. But we are equally opposed to any discrimination against or for a
man because of his creed. We demand that
all citizens, Protestant and Catholic, Jew and
Gentile, shall have fair treatment in every
way; that all alike shall have their rights
guaranteed them. The very reasons that
make us unqualified in our opposition to
State-aided sectarian schools make us equally
bent that, in the management of our public
schools, the adherents of each creed shall be
given exact and equal justice, wholly without regard to their religious affiliations; that
trustees, superintendents, teachers, scholars,
all alike, shall be treated without any reference whatsoever to the creed they profess.
We maintain that it is an outrage, in voting
for a man for any position, whether State
or national, to take into account his religious
faith, provided only he is a good American.
When a secret society does what in some
places the American Protective Association

seems to have done, and tries to proscribe
Catholics both politically and socially, the
members of such society show that they
themselves are as utterly un-American, as
alien to our school of political thought, as
the worst immigrants who land on our
shores. Their conduct is equally base and
contemptible; they are the worst foes of our
public-school system, because they strengthen
the hands of its ultramontane enemies; they
should receive the hearty condemnation of
all Americans who are truly patriotic.

The mighty tide of immigration to our
shores has brought in its train much of good
and much of evil; and whether the good
or the evil shall predominate depends mainly
on whether these newcomers do or do not
throw themselves heartily into our national
life, cease to be European, and become Americans like the rest of us. More than a third of
the people of the Northern States are of
foreign birth or parentage. An immense
number of them have become completely
Americanized, and these stand on exactly

the same plane as the descendants of any
Puritan, Cavalier, or Knickerbocker among
us, and do their full and honorable share of
the nation's work. But where immigrants
or the sons of immigrants, do not heartily
and in good faith throw in their lot with us,
but cling to the speech, the customs, the ways
of life, and the habits of thought of the Old
World which they have left, they thereby
harm both themselves and us. If they remain alien elements, unassimilated, and with
interests separate from ours, they are mere
obstructions to the current of our national
life, and, moreover, can get no good from it
themselves. In fact, though we ourselves
also suffer from their perversity, it is they
who really suffer most. It is an immense
benefit to the European immigrant to change
him into an American citizen. To bear the
name of American is to bear the most honorable of titles; and whoever does not so believe has no business to bear the name at all,
and, if he comes from Europe, the sooner he
goes back there the better. Besides, the man

who does not become Americanized nevertheless fails to remain a European, and becomes nothing at all. The immigrant cannot possibly remain what he was, or continue
to be a member of the Old-World society. If
he tries to retain his old language, in a few
generations it becomes a barbarous jargon;
if he tries to retain his old customs and ways
of life, in a few generations he becomes an
uncouth boor. He has cut himself off from
the Old-World, and cannot retain his con-
nection with it; and if he wishes ever to
amount to anything he must throw himself
heart and soul, and without reservation, into
the new life to which he has come. It is ur-
gently necessary to check and regulate our
immigration, by much more drastic laws than
now exist; and this should be done both to
keep out laborers who tend to depress the
labor market, and to keep out races which do
not assimilate readily with our own, and
unworthy individuals of all races—not only
criminals, idiots, and paupers, but anarchists
of the Most and O'Donovan Rossa type.

From his own standpoint, it is beyond all question the wise thing for the immigrant to become thoroughly Americanized. Moreover, from our standpoint, we have a right to demand it. We freely extend the hand of welcome and of good-fellowship to every man, no matter what his creed or birthplace, who comes here honestly intent on becoming a good United States citizen like the rest of us; but we have a right, and it is our duty to demand that he shall indeed become so, and shall not confuse the issues with which we are struggling by introducing among us Old-World quarrels and prejudices. There are certain ideas which he must give up. For instance, he must learn that American life is incompatible with the existence of any form of anarchy, or of any secret society having murder for its aim, whether at home or abroad; and he must learn that we exact full religious toleration and the complete separation of Church and State. Moreover, he must not bring in his Old-World religious race and national antipathies, but must merge

them into love for our common country, and
must take pride in the things which we can
all take pride in.   He must revere only our
flag ; not only must it come first, but no other
flag should even come second.   He must
learn to celebrate Washington's birthday
rather than that of the Queen or Kaiser, and
the Fourth of July instead of St. Patrick's
Day.   Our political and social questions must
be settled on their own merits, and not complicated by quarrels between England and
Ireland, or France and Germany, with which
we have nothing to do; it is an outrage to
fight an American political campaign with
reference to questions of European politics.
Above all, the immigrant must learn to talk
and think and *be* United States.

The immigrant of to-day can learn much
from the experience of the immigrants of
the past, who came to America prior to the
Revolutionary War.   We were then already,
what we are now, a people of mixed blood.
Many of our most illustrious Revolutionary
names were borne by men of Huguenot

blood—Jay, Sevier, Marion, Laurens. But
the Huguenots were, on the whole, the best
immigrants we have ever received; sooner
than any other, and more completely, they
became American in speech, conviction and
thought. The Hollanders took longer than
the Huguenots to become completely assimi-
lated; nevertheless they in the end became so,
immensely to their own advantage. One of
the leading Revolutionary generals, Schuyler, and one of the Presidents of the United
States, Van Buren, were of Dutch blood;
but they rose to their positions, the highest
in the land, because they had become Americans and had ceased being Hollanders. If
they had remained members of an alien body,
cut off by their speech and customs and belief from the rest of the American community, Schuyler would have lived his life
as a boorish, provincial squire, and Van
Buren would have ended his days a small
tavern-keeper. So it is with the Germans of
Pennsylvania. Those of them who became
Americanized have furnished to our history

a multitude of honorable names, from the days of the Mühlenbergs onward; but those who did not become Americanized form to the present day an unimportant body, of no significance in American existence. So it is with the Irish, who gave to Revolutionary annals such names as Carroll and Sullivan, and to the Civil war men like Sheridan—men who were Americans and nothing else: while the Irish who remain such, and busy themselves solely with alien politics, can have only an unhealthy influence upon American life, and can never rise as do their compatriots who become straightout Americans. Thus it has ever been with all people who have come hither, of whatever stock or blood. The same thing is true of the churches. A church which remains foreign, in language or spirit, is doomed.

But I wish to be distinctly understood on one point. Americanism is a question of spirit, conviction, and purpose, not of creed or birthplace. The politician who bids for the Irish or German vote, or the Irishman

or German who votes as an Irishman or
German, is despicable, for all citizens of this
commonwealth should vote solely as Americans; but he is not a whit less despicable than
the voter who votes against a good American, merely because that American happens
to have been born in Ireland or Germany.
Know-nothingism, in any form, is as utterly
un-American as foreignism. It is a base outrage to oppose a man because of his religion or birthplace, and all good citizens will
hold any such effort in abhorrence. A Scan-
dinavian, a German, or an Irishman who has
really become an American has the right to
stand on exactly the same footing as any native-born citizen in the land, and is just as
much entitled to the friendship and support,
social and political, of his neighbors. Among
the men with whom I have been thrown in
close personal contact socially, and who have
been among my staunchest friends and allies
politically, are not a few Americans who happen to have been born on the other side of
the water, in Germany, Ireland, Scandinavia;

and there could be no better men in the ranks of our native-born citizens.

In closing, I cannot better express the ideal attitude that should be taken by our fellow-citizens of foreign birth than by quoting the words of a representative American, born in Germany, the Honorable Richard Guenther. of Wisconsin. In a speech spoken at the time of the Samoan trouble, he said:

" We know as well as any other class of American citizens where our duties belong. We will work for our country in time of peace and fight for it in time of war, if a time of war should ever come. When I say our country, I mean, of course, our adopted country. I mean the United States of America. After passing through the crucible of naturalization, we are no longer Germans; we are Americans. Our attachment to America cannot be measured by the length of our residence here. We are Americans from the moment we touch the American shore until we are laid in American graves. We will fight for America whenever necessary. America, first, last, and all the time. America against Germany, America against the world; America, right or wrong; always America. We are Americans."

All honor to the man who spoke such words as those; and I believe they express the feelings of the great majority of those among our fellow-American citizens who were born abroad. We Americans can only do our allotted task well if we face it steadily and bravely, seeing but not fearing the dangers. Above all we must stand shoulder to shoulder, not asking as to the ancestry or creed of our comrades, but only demanding that they be in very truth Americans, and that we all work together, heart, hand, and head, for the honor and the greatness of our common country.

III

THE MANLY VIRTUES AND PRACTICAL POLITICS [1]

SOMETIMES, in addressing men who sincerely desire the betterment of our public affairs, but who have not taken active part in directing them, I feel tempted to tell them that there are two gospels which should be preached to every reformer. The first is the gospel of morality; the second is the gospel of efficiency.

To decent, upright citizens it is hardly necessary to preach the doctrine of morality as applied to the affairs of public life. It is an even graver offence to sin against the commonwealth than to sin against an individual. The man who debauches our public life, whether by malversation of funds in office,

[1] *The Forum*, July, 1894.

75

by the actual bribery of voters or of legislators, or by the corrupt use of the offices as
spoils wherewith to reward the unworthy
and the vicious for their noxious and interested activity in the baser walks of political
life,—this man is a greater foe to our well-
being as a nation than is even the defaulting
cashier of a bank, or the betrayer of a private trust.   No amount of intelligence and
no amount of energy will save a nation which
is not honest, and no government can ever
be a permanent success if administered in
accordance with base ideals.   The first req-
uisite in the citizen who wishes to share the
work of our public life, whether he wishes
himself to hold office or merely to do his
plain duty as an American by taking part in
the management of our political machinery,
is that he shall act disinterestedly and with
a sincere purpose to serve the whole commonwealth.

But disinterestedness and honesty and unselfish desire to do what is right are not enough
in themselves.   A man must not only be disin-

terested, but he must be efficient. If he goes into politics he must go into practical politics, in order to make his influence felt. Practical politics must not be construed to mean dirty politics. On the contrary, in the long run the politics of fraud and treachery and foulness are unpractical politics, and the most practical of all politicians is the politician who is clean and decent and upright. But a man who goes into the actual battles of the political world must prepare himself much as he would for the struggle in any other branch of our life. He must be prepared to meet men of far lower ideals than his own, and to face things, not as he would wish them, but as they are. He must not lose his own high ideal, and yet he must face the fact that the majority of the men with whom he must work have lower ideals. He must stand firmly for what he believes, and yet he must realize that political action, to be effective, must be the joint action of many men, and that he must sacrifice somewhat of his own opinions to those of his associates if he ever hopes to see his desires take practical shape.

The prime thing that every man who takes an interest in politics should remember is that he must act, and not merely criticise the actions of others. It is not the man who sits by his fireside reading his evening paper, and saying how bad our politics and politicians are, who will ever do anything to save us; it is the man who goes out into the rough hurly-burly of the caucus, the primary, and the political meeting, and there faces his fellows on equal terms. The real service is rendered, not by the critic who stands aloof from the contest, but by the man who enters into it and bears his part as a man should, undeterred by the blood and the sweat. It is a pleasant but a dangerous thing to associate merely with cultivated, refined men of high ideals and sincere purpose to do right, and to think that one has done all one's duty by discussing politics with such associates. It is a good thing to meet men of this stamp; indeed it is a necessary thing, for we thereby

brighten our ideals, and keep in touch with
the people who are unselfish in their purposes; but if we associate with such men
exclusively we can accomplish nothing. The
actual battle must be fought out on other and
less pleasant fields. The actual advance
must be made in the field of practical politics
among the men who represent or guide or
control the mass of the voters, the men who
are sometimes rough and coarse, who sometimes have lower ideals than they should, but
who are capable, masterful, and efficient. It
is only by mingling on equal terms with such
men, by showing them that one is able to
give and to receive heavy punishment without flinching, and that one can master the
details of political management as well as
they can, that it is possible for a man to establish a standing that will be useful to him
in fighting for a great reform. Every man
who wishes well to his country is in honor
bound to take an active part in political life.
If he does his duty and takes that active part
he will be sure occasionally to commit mis-

takes and to be guilty of shortcomings. For these mistakes and shortcomings he will receive the unmeasured denunciation of the critics who commit neither because they never do anything but criticise. Nevertheless he will have the satisfaction of knowing that the salvation of the country ultimately lies, not in the hands of his critics, but in the hands of those who, however imperfectly, actually do the work of the nation. I would not for one moment be understood as objecting to criticism or failing to appreciate its importance. We need fearless criticism of our public men and public parties; we need unsparing condemnation of all persons; and all principles that count for evil in our public life: but it behooves every man to remember that the work of the critic, important though it is, is of altogether secondary importance, and that, in the end, progress is accomplished by the man who does the things, and not by the man who talks about how they ought or ought not to be done.

Therefore the man who wishes to do good

in his community must go into active political life. If he is a Republican, let him join
his local Republican association; if a Democrat, the Democratic association; if an Independent, then let him put himself in touch
with those who think as he does. In any
event let him make himself an active force
and make his influence felt. Whether he
works within or without party lines he can
surely find plenty of men who are desirous of
good government, and who, if they act together, become at once a power on the side
of righteousness. Of course, in a government like ours, a man can accomplish anything only by acting in combination with
others, and equally, of course, a number of
people can act together only by each sacrificing certain of his beliefs or prejudices.
That man is indeed unfortunate who cannot
in any given district find some people with
whom he can conscientiously act. He may
find that he can do best by acting within
a party organization; he may find that he
can do best by acting, at least for certain

purposes, or at certain times, outside of party organizations, in an independent body of some kind; but with some association he must act if he wishes to exert any real influence.

One thing to be always remembered is that neither independence on the one hand nor party fealty on the other can ever be accepted as an excuse for failure to do active work in politics. The party man who offers his allegiance to party as an excuse for blindly following his party, right or wrong, and who fails to try to make that party in any way better, commits a crime against the country; and a crime quite as serious is committed by the independent who makes his independence an excuse for easy self-indulgence, and who thinks that when he says he belongs to neither party he is excused from the duty of taking part in the practical work of party organizations. The party man is bound to do his full share in party management. He is bound to attend the caucuses and the primaries, to see that only good

men are put up, and to exert his influence
as strenuously against the foes of good government within his party, as, through his
party machinery, he does against those who
are without the party. In the same way the
independent, if he cannot take part in the
regular organizations, is bound to do just
as much active constructive work (not merely
the work of criticism) outside; he is bound
to try to get up an organization of his own
and to try to make that organization felt in
some effective manner. Whatever course
the man who wishes to do his duty by his
country takes in reference to parties or to independence of parties, he is bound to try to
put himself in touch with men who think as
he does, and to help make their joint influence felt in behalf of the powers that go for
decency and good government. He must try
to accomplish things; he must not vote in the
air unless it is really necessary. Occasionally a man must cast a " conscience vote,"
when there is no possibility of carrying to
victory his principles or his nominees; at

times, indeed, this may be his highest duty; but ordinarily this is not the case. As a general rule a man ought to work and vote for something which there is at least a fair chance of putting into effect.

Yet another thing to be remembered by the man who wishes to make his influence felt for good in our politics is that he must act purely as an American. If he is not deeply imbued with the American spirit he cannot succeed. Any organization which tries to work along the line of caste or creed, which fails to treat all American citizens on their merits as men, will fail, and will deserve to fail. Where our political life is healthy, there is and can be no room for any movement organized to help or to antagonize men because they do or do not profess a certain religion, or because they were or were not born here or abroad. We have a right to ask that those with whom we associate, and those for whom we vote, shall be themselves good Americans in heart and spirit, unhampered by adherence to foreign ideals, and act-

ing without regard to the national and religious prejudices of European countries; but
if they really are good Americans in spirit
and thought and purpose, that is all that we
have any right to consider in regard to them.
In the same way there must be no discrimination for or against any man because of his
social standing. On the one side, there is
nothing to be made out of a political organization which draws an exclusive social line,
and on the other it must be remembered that
it is just as un-American to vote against a
man because he is rich as to vote against him
because he is poor. The one man has just
as much right as the other to claim to be
treated purely on his merits as a man. In
short, to do good work in politics, the men
who organize must organize wholly without
regard to whether their associates were born
here or abroad, whether they are Protestants
or Catholics, Jews or Gentiles, whether they
are bankers or butchers, professors or day-
laborers. All that can rightly be asked of
one's political associates is that they shall be

honest men, good Americans, and substantially in accord as regards their political ideas.

Another thing that must not be forgotten by the man desirous of doing good political work is the need of the rougher, manlier virtues, and above all the virtue of personal courage, physical as well as moral. If we wish to do good work for our country, we must be unselfish, disinterested, sincerely desirous of the well being of the commonwealth, and capable of devoted adherence to a lofty ideal; but in addition we must be vigorous in mind and body, able to hold our own in rough conflict with our fellows, able to suffer punishment without flinching, and, at need, to repay it in kind with full interest. A peaceful and commercial civilization is always in danger of suffering the loss of the virile fighting qualities without which no nation, however cultured, however refined, however thrifty and prosperous, can ever amount to anything. Every citizen should be taught, both in public and in private life,

that while he must avoid brawling and quar-
relling, it is his duty to stand up for his
rights. He must realize that the only man
who is more contemptible than the blusterer
and bully is the coward. No man is worth
much to the commonwealth if he is not capable of feeling righteous wrath and just indignation, if he is not stirred to hot anger by
misdoing, and is not impelled to see justice
meted out to the wrongdoers. No man is
worth much anywhere if he does not possess both moral and physical courage. A
politician who really serves his country well,
and deserves his country's gratitude, must
usually possess some of the hardy virtues
which we admire in the soldier who serves
his country well in the field.

An ardent young reformer is very apt to
try to begin by reforming too much. He
needs always to keep in mind that he has got
to serve as a sergeant before he assumes the
duties of commander-in-chief. It is right
for him from the beginning to take a great
interest in National, State, and Municipal af-

fairs, and to try to make himself felt in them if the occasion arises; but the best work must be done by the citizen working in his own ward or district. Let him associate himself with the men who think as he does, and who, like him, are sincerely devoted to the public good. Then let them try to make themselves felt in the choice of alderman, of councilman, of assemblyman. The politicians will be prompt to recognize their power, and the people will recognize it too, after a while. Let them organize and work, undaunted by any temporary defeat. If they fail at first, and if they fail again, let them merely make up their minds to redouble their efforts, and perhaps alter their methods; but let them keep on working.

It is sheer unmanliness and cowardice to shrink from the contest because at first there is failure, or because the work is difficult or repulsive. No man who is worth his salt has any right to abandon the effort to better our politics merely because he does not find it pleasant, merely because it entails associations which to him happen to be disagreeable. Let him keep right on, taking the buffets he gets good-humoredly, and repaying them with heartiness when the chance arises. Let him make up his mind that he will have to face the violent opposition of the spoils politician, and also, too often, the unfair and ungenerous criticism of those who ought to know better. Let him be careful not to show himself so thin-skinned as to mind either; let him fight his way forward, paying only so much regard to both as is necessary to enable him to win in spite of them. He may not, and indeed probably will not, accomplish nearly as much as he would like to, or as he thinks he ought to: but he will certainly accomplish something; and if he can feel that he has helped to elevate the type of representative sent to the municipal, the State, or the national legislature from his district, or to elevate the standard of duty among the public officials in his own ward, he has a right to be profoundly satisfied with what he has accomplished.

Finally, there is one other matter which the man who tries to wake his fellows to higher political action would do well to ponder. It is a good thing to appeal to citizens to work for good government because it will better their estate materially, but it is a far better thing to appeal to them to work for good government because it is right in itself to do so. Doubtless, if we can have clean honest politics, we shall be better off in material matters. A thoroughly pure, upright, and capable administration of the affairs of New York city results in a very appreciable increase of comfort to each citizen. We should have better systems of transportation; we should have cleaner streets, better sewers, and the like. But it is sometimes difficult to show the individual citizen that he will be individually better off in his business and in his home affairs for taking part in politics. I do not think it is always worth while to show that this will always be the case. The citizen should be appealed to primarily on the ground that it is his plain duty, if he wishes

to deserve the name of freeman, to do his
full share in the hard and difficult work of
self-government. He must do his share unless he is willing to prove himself unfit for
free institutions, fit only to live under a government where he will be plundered and bullied because he deserves to be plundered and
bullied on account of his selfish timidity and
short-sightedness. A clean and decent government is sure in the end to benefit our citizens in the material circumstances of their
lives; but each citizen should be appealed to,
to take part in bettering our politics, not for
the sake of any possible improvement it may
bring to his affairs, but on the ground that
it is his plain duty to do so, and that this is a
duty which it is cowardly and dishonorable
in him to shirk.

To sum up, then, the men who wish to
work for decent politics must work practically, and yet must not swerve from their devotion to a high ideal. They must actually
do things, and not merely confine themselves
to criticising those who do them. They must

work disinterestedly, and appeal to the disinterested element in others, although they must also do work which will result in the material betterment of the community. They must act as Americans through and through, in spirit and hope and purpose, and, while being disinterested, unselfish, and generous in their dealings with others, they must also show that they possess the essential manly virtues of energy, of resolution, and of indomitable personal courage.

IV

THE COLLEGE GRADUATE
AND PUBLIC LIFE [1]

THERE are always, in our national life, certain tendencies that give us ground for alarm, and certain others that give us ground for hope. Among the latter we must put the fact that there has undoubtedly been a growing feeling among educated men that they are in honor bound to do their full share of the work of American public life.

We have in this country an equality of rights. It is the plain duty of every man to see that his rights are respected. That weak good-nature which acquiesces in wrong-doing, whether from laziness, timidity, or indifference, is a very unwholesome quality. It should be second nature with every man to

[1] *Atlantic Monthly*, August, 1894.

insist that he be given full justice. But if there is an equality of rights, there is an inequality of duties. It is proper to demand more from the man with exceptional advantages than from the man without them. A heavy moral obligation rests upon the man of means and upon the man of education to do their full duty by their country. On no class does this obligation rest more heavily than upon the men with a collegiate education, the men who are graduates of our universities. Their education gives them no right to feel the least superiority over any of their fellow-citizens; but it certainly ought to make them feel that they should stand foremost in the honorable effort to serve the whole public by doing their duty as Americans in the body politic. This obligation very possibly rests even more heavily upon the men of means; but of this it is not necessary now to speak. The men of mere wealth never can have and never should have the capacity for doing good work that is possessed by the men of exceptional mental training; but that they may become both a laughing-stock and a menace to the community is made unpleasantly apparent by that portion of the New York business and social world which is most in evidence in the newspapers.

To the great body of men who have had exceptional advantages in the way of educational facilities we have a right, then, to look for good service to the state. The service may be rendered in many different ways. In a reasonable number of cases, the man may himself rise to high political position. That men actually do so rise is shown by the number of graduates of Harvard, Yale, and our other universities who are now taking a prominent part in public life. These cases must necessarily, however, form but a small part of the whole. The enormous majority of our educated men have to make their own living, and are obliged to take up careers in which they must work heart and soul to succeed. Nevertheless, the man of business and the man of science, the doctor of divinity and the doctor of law, the architect, the engineer, and the writer, all alike owe a positive duty to the community, the neglect of which they cannot excuse on any plea of their private affairs. They are bound to follow understandingly the course of public events; they are bound to try to estimate and form judgment upon public men; and they are bound to act intelligently and effectively in support of the principles which they deem to be right and for the best interests of the country.

The most important thing for this class of educated men to realize is that they do not really form a class at all. I have used the word in default of another, but I have merely used it roughly to group together people who have had unusual opportunities of a certain kind. A large number of the people to whom these opportunities are offered fail to take advantage of them, and a very much larger number of those to whom they have not been offered succeed none the less in making them for themselves. An educated man must not go into politics as such; he must go in simply as an American; and when he is once in, he will speedily realize that he must work very hard indeed, or he will be upset by some other American, with no education at all, but with much natural capacity. His education ought to make him feel particularly ashamed of himself if he acts meanly or dishonorably, or in any way falls short of the ideal of good citizenship, and it ought to make him feel that he must show that he has profited by it; but it should certainly give him no feeling of superiority until by actual work he has shown that superiority. In other words, the educated man must realize that he is living in a democracy and under democratic conditions, and that he is entitled to no more respect and consideration than he can win by actual performance.

This must be steadily kept in mind not only by educated men themselves, but particularly by the men who give the tone to our great educational institutions. These educational institutions, if they are to do their best work, must strain every effort to keep their life in touch with the life of the nation at the present day. This is necessary for the country, but it is very much more necessary for the educated men themselves. It is a misfortune for any land if its people of cultivation take little part in shaping its destiny; but the misfortune is far greater for the people of cultivation. The country has a right to demand the honest and efficient service of every man in it, but especially of every man who has had the advantage of rigid mental and moral training; the country is so much the poorer when any class of honest men fail to do their duty by it; but the loss to the class itself is immeasurable. If our educated men as a whole become incapable of playing their full part in our life, if they cease doing their share of the rough, hard work which must be done, and grow to take a position of mere dilettanteism in our public affairs, they will speedily sink in relation to their fellows who really do the work of governing, until they stand toward them as a cultivated, ineffective man with a taste for bric-a-brac stands toward a great artist. When once a body of citizens becomes thoroughly out of touch and out of temper with the national life, its usefulness is gone, and its power of leaving its mark on the times is gone also.

The first great lesson which the college graduate should learn is the lesson of work rather than of criticism. Criticism is necessary and useful; it is often indispensable; but it can never take the place of action, or be even a poor substitute for it. The function of the mere critic is of very subordinate usefulness. It is the doer of deeds who actually counts in the battle for life, and not the man who looks on and says how the fight ought to be fought, without himself sharing the stress and the danger.

There is, however, a need for proper critical work. Wrongs should be strenuously and fearlessly denounced; evil principles and evil men should be condemned. The politician who cheats or swindles, or the newspaper man who lies in any form, should be made to feel that he is an object of scorn for all honest men. We need fearless criticism; but we need that it should also be intelligent. At present, the man who is most apt to regard himself as an intelligent critic of our political affairs is often the man who knows nothing whatever about them. Criticism which is ignorant or prejudiced is a source of great harm to the nation; and where ignorant or prejudiced critics are themselves educated men, their attitude does real harm also to the class to which they belong.

The tone of a portion of the press of the country toward public men, and especially toward political opponents, is degrading, all forms of coarse and noisy slander being apparently considered legitimate weapons to employ against men of the opposite party or faction. Unfortunately, not a few of the journals that pride themselves upon being independent in politics, and the organs of cultivated men, betray the same characteristics in a less coarse but quite as noxious form. All these journals do great harm by accustoming good citizens to see

their public men, good and bad, assailed in-
discriminately as scoundrels. The effect is
twofold: the citizen learning, on the one
hand, to disbelieve any statement he sees in
any newspaper, so that the attacks on evil
lose their edge; and on the other, gradually
acquiring a deep-rooted belief that all public
men are more or less bad. In consequence,
his political instinct becomes hopelessly
blurred, and he grows unable to tell the good
representative from the bad. The worst offence that can be committed against the Republic is the offence of the public man who
betrays his trust; but second only to it comes
the offence of the man who tries to persuade
others that an honest and efficient public man
is dishonest or unworthy. This is a wrong
that can be committed in a great many different ways. Downright foul abuse may be, after all, less dangerous than incessant mis-
statements, sneers, and those half-truths
that are the meanest lies.

For educated men of weak fibre, there lies
a real danger in that species of literary work

which appeals to their cultivated senses because of its scholarly and pleasant tone, but
which enjoins as the proper attitude to as-
sume in public life one of mere criticism and
negation; which teaches the adoption toward
public men and public affairs of that sneer-
ing tone which so surely denotes a mean and
small mind. If a man does not have belief
and enthusiasm, the chances are small indeed that he will ever do a man's work in
the world; and the paper or the college
which, by its general course, tends to eradi-
cate this power of belief and enthusiasm, this
desire for work, has rendered to the young
men under its influence the worst service it
could possibly render. Good can often be
done by criticising sharply and severely the
wrong; but excessive indulgence in criticism
is never anything but bad, and no amount of
criticism can in any way take the place of
active and zealous warfare for the right.

Again, there is a certain tendency in college life, a tendency encouraged by some of
the very papers referred to, to make educated

men shrink from contact with the rough people who do the world's work, and associate only with one another and with those who think as they do. This is a most dangerous tendency. It is very agreeable to deceive one's self into the belief that one is performing the whole duty of man by sitting at home in ease, doing nothing wrong, and confining one's participation in politics to conversations and meetings with men who have had the same training and look at things in the same way. It is always a temptation to do this, because those who do nothing else often speak as if in some way they deserved credit for their attitude, and as if they stood above their brethren who plough the rough fields. Moreover, many people whose political work is done more or less after this fashion are very noble and very sincere in their aims and aspirations, and are striving for what is best and most decent in public life.

Nevertheless, this is a snare round which it behooves every young man to walk carefully. Let him beware of associating only with the people of his own caste and of his own little ways of political thought. Let him learn that he must deal with the mass of men; that he must go out and stand shoulder to shoulder with his friends of every rank, and face to face with his foes of every rank, and must bear himself well in the hurly-burly. He must not be frightened by the many unpleasant features of the contest, and he must not expect to have it all his own way, or to accomplish too much. He will meet with checks and will make many mistakes; but if he perseveres, he will achieve a measure of success and will do a measure of good such as is never possible to the refined, cultivated, intellectual men who shrink aside from the actual fray.

Yet again, college men must learn to be as practical in politics as they would be in business or in law. It is surely unnecessary to say that by "practical" I do not mean anything that savors in the least of dishonesty. On the contrary, a college man is peculiarly bound to keep a high ideal and to be true to it; but he must work in practical ways to try to realize this ideal, and must not refuse to do anything because he cannot get everything. One especially necessary thing is to know the facts by actual experience, and not to take refuge in mere theorizing. There are always a number of excellent and well-meaning men whom we grow to regard with amused impatience because they waste all their energies on some visionary scheme which, even if it were not visionary, would be useless. When they come to deal with political questions, these men are apt to err from sheer lack of familiarity with the workings of our government. No man ever really learned from books how to manage a governmental system. Books are admirable adjuncts, and the statesman who has carefully studied them is far more apt to do good work than if he had not; but if he has never done anything but study books he will not be a statesman at all. Thus, every young politician should of course read the *Federalist*. It is the greatest book of the kind that has ever been written. Hamilton, Madison, and Jay would have been poorly equipped for writing it if they had not possessed an extensive acquaintance with literature, and in particular if they had not been careful students of political literature; but the great cause of the value of their writings lay in the fact that they knew by actual work and association what practical politics meant. They had helped to shape the political thought of the country, and to do its legislative and executive work, and so they were in a condition to speak understandingly about it. For similar reasons, Mr. Bryce's *American Commonwealth* has a value possessed by no other book of the kind, largely because Mr. Bryce is himself an active member of Parliament, a man of good standing and some leadership in his own party, and a practical politician. In the same way, a life of Washington by Cabot Lodge, a sketch of Lincoln by Carl Schurz, a biography of Pitt by Lord Rosebery, have an added value because of the writers' own work in politics.

It is always a pity to see men fritter away their energies on any pointless scheme; and unfortunately, a good many of our educated people when they come to deal with politics, do just such frittering. Take, for instance, the queer freak of arguing in favor of establishing what its advocates are pleased to call " responsible government " in our institutions, or in other words of grafting certain features of the English parliamentary system upon our own Presidential and Congressional system. This agitation was too largely deficient in body to enable it to last, and it has now, I think, died away; but at one time quite a number of our men who spoke of themselves as students of political history were engaged in treating this scheme as something serious. Few men who had ever taken an active part in politics, or who had studied politics in the way that a doctor is expected to study surgery and medicine, so much as gave it a thought; but very intelligent men did, just because they were misdirecting their energies, and were wholly ignorant that they ought to know practically about a problem before they attempted its solution. The English, or so-called "responsible," theory of parliamentary government is one entirely incompatible with our own governmental institutions. It could not be put into operation here save by absolutely sweeping away the United States Constitution. Incidentally, I may say it would be to the last degree undesirable, if it were practicable. But this is not the point upon which I wish to dwell; the point is that it was wholly impracticable to put it into operation, and that an agitation favoring this kind of government was from its nature unintelligent. The people who wrote about it wasted their time, whereas they could have spent it to great advantage had they seriously studied our institutions and sought to devise practicable and desirable methods of increasing and centering genuine responsibility—for all thinking men agree that there is an undoubted need for a change in this direction.

But of course much of the best work that has been done in the field of political study has been done by men who were not active politicians, though they were careful and painstaking students of the phenomena of politics. The back numbers of our leading magazines afford proof of this. Certain of the governmental essays by such writers as Mr. Lawrence Lowell and Professor A. B. Hart, and especially such books as that on the *Speakers' Powers and Duties,* by Miss Follet, have been genuine and valuable contributions to our political thought. These essays have been studied carefully not only by scholars, but by men engaged in practical politics, because they were written with good judgment and keen insight after careful investigation of the facts, and so deserved respectful attention.

It is a misfortune for any people when the paths of the practical and the theoretical politicians diverge so widely that they have no common standing-ground. When the Greek thinkers began to devote their attention to purely visionary politics of the kind found in Plato's Republic, while the Greek practical politicians simply exploited the quarrelsome little commonwealths in their own interests, then the end of Greek liberty was at hand. No government that cannot command the respectful support of the best thinkers is in an entirely sound condition; but it is well to keep in mind the remark of Frederick the Great, that if he wished to punish a province, he would allow it to be governed by the philosophers. It is a great misfortune for the country when the practical politician and the doctrinaire have no point in common, but the misfortune is, if anything, greatest for the doctrinaire. The ideal to be set before the student of politics and the practical politician alike is the ideal of the *Federalist*. Each man should realize that he cannot do his best, either in the study of politics or in applied politics unless he has a working knowledge of both branches. A limited number of people can do good work by the careful study of governmental institutions, but they can do it only if they have themselves a practical knowledge of the workings of these institutions. A very large number of people, on the other hand, may do excellent work in politics without much theoretic knowledge of the subject; but without this knowledge they cannot rise to the highest rank, while in any rank their capacity to do good work will be immensely increased if they have such knowledge.

There are certain other qualities, about which it is hardly necessary to speak. If an educated man is not heartily American in instinct and feeling and taste and sympathy, he will amount to nothing in our public life. Patriotism, love of country, and pride in the flag which symbolizes country may be feelings which the race will at some period outgrow, but at present they are very real and strong, and the man who lacks them is a useless creature, a mere incumbrance to the land.

A man of sound political instincts can no

more subscribe to the doctrine of absolute
independence of party on the one hand than
to that of unquestioning party allegiance on
the other. No man can accomplish much
unless he works in an organization with
others, and this organization, no matter how
temporary, is a party for the time being.
But that man is a dangerous citizen who so
far mistakes means for ends as to become
servile in his devotion to his party, and
afraid to leave it when the party goes wrong.
To deify either independence or party allegiance merely as such is a little absurd. It
depends entirely upon the motive, the purpose, the result. For the last two years, the
Senator who, beyond all his colleagues in
the United States Senate, has shown himself
independent of party ties is the very man
to whom the leading champions of independence in politics most strenuously object.
The truth is, simply, that there are times
when it may be the duty of a man to break
with his party, and there are other times
when it may be his duty to stand by his

party, even though, on some points, he thinks that party wrong; he must be prepared to leave it when necessary, and he must not sacrifice his influence by leaving it unless it is necessary. If we had no party allegiance, our politics would become mere windy anarchy, and, under present conditions, our government could hardly continue at all. If we had no independence, we should always be running the risk of the most degraded kind of despotism,—the despotism of the party boss and the party machine.

It is just the same way about compromises. Occasionally one hears some well-meaning person say of another, apparently in praise, that he is " never willing to compromise." It is a mere truism to say that, in politics, there has to be one continual compromise. Of course now and then questions arise upon which a compromise is inadmissible. There could be no compromise with secession, and there was none. There should be no avoidable compromise about any great moral question. But only a few great reforms or great measures of any kind can be carried through without concession. No student of American history needs to be reminded that the Constitution itself is a bundle of compromises, and was adopted only because of this fact, and that the same thing is true of the Emancipation Proclamation.

In conclusion, then, the man with a university education is in honor bound to take an active part in our political life, and to do his full duty as a citizen by helping his fellow-citizens to the extent of his power in the exercise of the rights of self-government. He is bound to rank action far above criticism, and to understand that the man deserving of credit is the man who actually does the things, even though imperfectly, and not the man who confines himself to talking about how they ought to be done. He is bound to have a high ideal and to strive to realize it, and yet he must make up his mind that he will never be able to get the highest good, and that he must devote himself with all his energy to getting the best that he can. Finally, his work must be disinterested and honest, and it must be given without regard to his own success or failure, and without regard to the effect it has upon his own fortunes; and while he must show the virtues of uprightness and tolerance and gentleness, he must also show the sterner virtues of courage, resolution, and hardihood, and the desire to war with merciless effectiveness against the existence of wrong.

V

PHASES OF STATE LEGIS-
LATION [1]

THE ALBANY LEGISLATURE.

FEW persons realize the magnitude of
the interests affected by State legislation in New York. It is no mere figure of
speech to call New York the Empire State;
and many of the laws most directly and immediately affecting the interests of its citizens are passed at Albany, and not at Washington. In fact, there is at Albany a little
home rule parliament which presides over
the destinies of a commonwealth more pop-
ulous than any one of two thirds of the
kingdoms of Europe, and one which, in
point of wealth, material prosperity, variety
of interests, extent of territory, and capacity

[1] The *Century*, January, 1885.

for expansion, can fairly be said to rank next to the powers of the first class. This little parliament, composed of one hundred and twenty-eight members in the Assembly and thirty-two in the Senate, is, in the fullest sense of the term, a *representative* body; there is hardly one of the many and widely diversified interests of the State that has not a mouthpiece at Albany, and hardly a single class of its citizens—not even excepting, I regret to say, the criminal class—which lacks its representative among the legislators. In the three Legislatures of which I have been a member, I have sat with bankers and bricklayers, with merchants and mechanics, with lawyers, farmers, day-laborers, saloon-keepers, clergymen, and prize-fighters. Among my colleagues there were many very good men; there was a still more numerous class of men who were neither very good nor very bad, but went one way or the other, according to the strength of the various con-flicting influences acting around, behind, and upon them; and, finally, there were many

very bad men. Still, the New York Legislature, taken as a whole, is by no means as bad
a body as we would be led to believe if our
judgment was based purely on what we read
in the great metropolitan papers; for the
custom of the latter is to portray things as
either very much better or very much worse
than they are. Where a number of men,
many of them poor, some of them unscrupulous, and others elected by constituents too
ignorant to hold them to a proper account-
ability for their actions, are put into a position of great temporary power, where they
are called to take action upon questions affecting the welfare of large corporations and
wealthy private individuals, the chances for
corruption are always great; and that there
is much viciousness and political dishonesty,
much moral cowardice, and a good deal of
actual bribe-taking in Albany, no one who
has had any practical experience of legislation can doubt; but, at the same time, I think
that the good members generally outnumber
the bad, and that there is not often doubt as

to the result when a naked question of right or wrong can be placed clearly and in its true light before the Legislature. The trouble is that on many questions the Legislature never does have the right and wrong clearly shown it. Either some bold, clever parliamentary tactician snaps the measure through before the members are aware of its nature, or else the obnoxious features are so combined with good ones as to procure the support of a certain proportion of that large class of men whose intentions are excellent, but whose intellects are foggy. Or else the necessary party organization, which we call the "machine," uses its great power for some definite evil aim.

THE CHARACTER OF THE REPRESENTATIVES.

THE representatives from different sections of the State differ widely in character. Those from the country districts are generally very good men. They are usually well-to-do farmers, small lawyers, or prosperous store-keepers, and are shrewd, quiet, and honest. They are often narrow-minded

and slow to receive an idea; but, on the
other hand, when they get a good one, they
cling to it with the utmost tenacity. They
form very much the most valuable class of
legislators. For the most part they are native Americans, and those who are not are
men who have become completely Americanized in all their ways and habits of thought.
One of the most useful members of the last
Legislature was a German from a western
county, and the extent of his Americaniza-
tion can be judged from the fact that he was
actually an ardent prohibitionist: certainly
no one who knows Teutonic human nature
will require further proof. Again, I sat for
an entire session beside a very intelligent
member from northern New York before I
discovered that he was an Irishman: all his
views of legislation, even upon such subjects
as free schools and the impropriety of making appropriations from the treasury for
the support of sectarian institutions, were
precisely similar to those of his Protestant-
American neighbors, though he was himself

a Catholic. Now a German or an Irishman from one of the great cities would probably have retained many of his national peculiarities.

It is from these same great cities that the worst legislators come. It is true that there are always among them a few cultivated and scholarly men who are well educated, and who stand on a higher and broader intellectual and moral plane than the country members, but the bulk are very low indeed. They are usually foreigners, of little or no education, with exceedingly misty ideas as to morality, and possessed of an ignorance so profound that it could only be called comic, were it not for the fact that it has at times such serious effects upon our laws. It is their ignorance, quite as much as actual viciousness, which makes it so difficult to procure the passage of good laws or prevent the passage of bad ones; and it is the most irritating of the many elements with which we have to contend in the fight for good government.

DARK SIDE OF THE LEGISLATIVE PICTURE.

MENTION has been made above of the bribe-taking which undoubtedly at times occurs in the New York Legislature. This is what is commonly called "a delicate subject" with which to deal, and, therefore, according to our usual methods of handling delicate subjects, it is either never discussed at all, or else discussed with the grossest exaggeration; but most certainly there is nothing about which it is more important to know the truth.

In each of the last three legislatures there were a number of us who were interested in getting through certain measures which we deemed to be for the public good, but which were certain to be strongly opposed, some for political and some for pecuniary reasons. Now, to get through any such measure requires genuine hard work, a certain amount of parliamentary skill, a good deal of tact and courage, and above all, a thorough knowledge of the men with whom one has to deal, and of the motives which actuate them. In other words, before taking any active steps, we had to " size up " our fellow-legislators, to find out their past history and present character and associates, to find out whether they were their own masters or were acting under the directions of somebody else, whether they were bright or stupid, etc., etc. As a result, and after very careful study, conducted purely with the object of learning the truth, so that we might work more effectually, we came to the conclusion that about a third of the members were open to corrupt influences in some form or other; in certain sessions the proportion was greater, and in some less. Now it would, of course, be impossible for me or for anyone else to prove in a court of law that these men were guilty, except perhaps in two or three cases; yet we felt absolutely confident that there was hardly a case in which our judgment as to the honesty of any given member was not correct. The two or three exceptional cases alluded to, where legal proof of guilt might have been forthcoming, were instances in which honest men were approached by their colleagues at times when the need for votes was very great; but, even then, it would have been almost impossible to punish the offenders before a court, for it would have merely resulted in his denying what his accuser stated. Moreover, the members who had been approached would have been very reluctant to come forward, for each of them felt ashamed that his character should not have been well enough known to prevent anyone's daring to speak to him on such a subject. And another reason why the few honest men who are approached (for the lobbyist rarely makes a mistake in his estimate of the men who will be apt to take bribes) do not feel like taking action in the matter is that a doubtful lawsuit will certainly follow, which will drag on so long that the public will come to regard all of the participants with equal distrust, while in the end the decision is quite as likely to be against as to be for them. Take the Bradley-Sessions case, for ex-

ample. This was an incident that occurred
at the time of the faction-fight in the Republican ranks over the return of Mr. Conkling
to the United States Senate after his resig-
nation from that body. Bradley, an Assemblyman, accused Sessions, a State Senator, of attempting to bribe him. The affair
dragged on for an indefinite time; no one
was able actually to determine whether it
was a case of blackmail on the one hand, or
of bribery on the other; the vast majority
of people recollected the names of both
parties, but totally forgot which it was that
was supposed to have bribed the other, and
regarded both with equal disfavor; and the
upshot has been that the case is now merely
remembered as illustrating one of the most
unsavory phases of the once-famous Half-
breed-Stalwart fight.

DIFFICULTIES OF PREVENTING AND PUNISH-ING CORRUPTION.

FROM the causes indicated, it is almost impossible to actually convict a legislator of

bribe-taking; but at the same time, the character of a legislator, if bad, soon becomes a matter of common notoriety, and no dishonest legislator can long keep his reputation good with honest men. If the constituents wish to know the character of their member, they can easily find it out, and no member will be dishonest if he thinks his constituents are looking at him; he presumes upon their ignorance or indifference. I do not see how bribe-taking among legislators can be stopped until the public conscience becomes awake to the matter. Then it will stop fast enough; for just as soon as politicians realize that the people are in earnest in wanting a thing done, they make haste to do it. The trouble is always in rousing the people sufficiently to make them take an *effective* interest,—that is, in making them sufficiently in earnest to be willing to give a little of their time to the accomplishment of the object they have in view.

Much the largest percentage of corrupt legislators come from the great cities; in-

deed, the majority of the assemblymen from
the great cities are "very poor specimens"
indeed, while, on the contrary, the congress-
men who go from them are generally pretty
good men. This fact is only one of the
many which go to establish the curious political law that in a great city the larger the
constituency which elects a public servant,
the more apt that servant is to be a good
one; exactly as the Mayor is almost certain
to be infinitely superior in character to the
average alderman, or the average city judge
to the average civil justice. This is because
the public servants, of comparatively small
importance are protected by their own in-
significance from the consequences of their
bad actions. Life is carried on at such a high
pressure in the great cities, men's time is so
fully occupied by their manifold and harassing interests and duties, and their knowledge
of their neighbors is necessarily so limited,
that they are only able to fix in their minds
the characters and records of a few prominent men; the others they lump together

without distinguishing between individuals.
They know whether the aldermen, as a body,
are to be admired or despised; but they probably do not even know the name, far less
the worth, of the particular alderman who
represents their district; so it happens that
their votes for aldermen or assemblymen are
generally given with very little intelligence
indeed, while, on the contrary, they are fully
competent to pass and execute judgment
upon as prominent an official as a mayor or
even a congressman. Hence it follows that
the latter have to give a good deal of attention to the wishes and prejudices of the
public at large, while a city assemblyman,
though he always talks a great deal about
the people, rarely, except in certain extraordinary cases, has to pay much heed to their
wants. His political future depends far more
upon the skill and success with which he
cultivates the good-will of certain " bosses,"
or of certain cliques of politicians, or even of
certain bodies and knots of men (such as
compose a trade-union, or a collection of mer-

chants in some special business, or the managers of a railroad) whose interests, being vitally affected by Albany legislation, oblige them closely to watch, and to try to punish or reward, the Albany legislators. These politicians or sets of interested individuals generally care very little for a man's honesty so long as he can be depended upon to do as they wish on certain occasions; and hence it often happens that a dishonest man who has sense enough not to excite attention by any flagrant outrage may continue for a number of years to represent an honest constituency.

THE CONSTITUENTS LARGELY TO BLAME.

MOREOVER, a member from a large city can often count upon the educated and intelligent men of his district showing the most gross ignorance and stupidity in political affairs. The much-lauded intelligent voter— the man of cultured mind, liberal education, and excellent intentions—at times performs exceedingly queer antics.

The great public meetings to advance certain political movements irrespective of party, which have been held so frequently during the past few years, have undoubtedly done a vast amount of good; but the very men who attend these public meetings and inveigh against the folly and wickedness of the politicians will sometimes on election day do things which have quite as evil effects as any of the acts of the men whom they very properly condemn. A recent instance of this is worth giving. In 1882 there was in the Assembly a young member from New York, who did as hard and effective work for the city of New York as has ever been done by anyone. It was a peculiarly disagreeable year to be in the Legislature. The composition of that body was unusually bad. The more disreputable politicians relied upon it to pass some of their schemes and to protect certain of their members from the consequences of their own misdeeds. Demagogic measures were continually brought forward, nominally in the interests of the laboring

classes, for which an honest and intelligent
man could not vote, and yet which were jeal-
ously watched by, and received the hearty
support of, not mere demagogues and agitators, but also a large number of perfectly
honest though misguided workingmen. And,
finally, certain wealthy corporations attempted, by the most unscrupulous means,
to rush through a number of laws in their
own interest. The young member of whom
we are speaking incurred by his course on
these various measures the bitter hostility
alike of the politicians, the demagogues, and
the members of that most dangerous of all
classes, the wealthy criminal class. He had
also earned the gratitude of all honest citizens, and he got it—as far as words went.
The better class of newspapers spoke well
of him; cultured and intelligent men generally—the well-to-do, prosperous people
who belong to the different social and literary clubs, and their followers—were loud in
his praise. I call to mind one man who lived
in his district who expressed great indigna-

tion that the politicians should dare to oppose his re-election; when told that it was
to be hoped he would help to insure the legislator's return to Albany by himself staying
at the polls all day, he answered that he was
very sorry, but he unfortunately had an en-
gagement to go quail-shooting on election
day! Most respectable people, however,
would undoubtedly have voted for and re-
elected the young member had it not been
for the unexpected political movements that
took place in the fall. A citizen's ticket,
largely non-partisan in character, was run
for certain local offices, receiving its support
from among those who claimed to be, and
who undoubtedly were, the best men of both
parties. The ticket contained the names of
candidates only for municipal offices, and
had nothing whatever to do with the election
of men to the Legislature; yet it proved absolutely impossible to drill this simple fact
through the heads of a great many worthy
people, who, when election day came round,
declined to vote anything but the citizens'

ticket, and persisted in thinking that if no legislative candidate was on the ticket, it was because, for some reason or other, the citizens' committee did not consider any legislative candidate worth voting for. All over the city the better class of candidates for legislative offices lost from this cause votes which they had a right to expect, and in the particular district under consideration the loss was so great as to cause the defeat of the sitting member, or rather to elect him by so narrow a vote as to enable an unscrupulously partisan legislative majority to keep him out of his seat.

It is this kind of ignorance of the simplest political matters among really good citizens, combined with their timidity, which is so apt to characterize a wealthy *bourgeoisie*, and with their short-sighted selfishness in being unwilling to take the smallest portion of time away from their business or pleasure to devote to public affairs, which renders it so easy for corrupt men from the city to keep their places in the Legislature. In the country

the case is different. Here the constituencies,
who are usually composed of honest though
narrow-minded and bigoted individuals, generally keep a pretty sharp lookout on their
members, and, as already said, the latter are
apt to be fairly honest men. Even when they
are not honest, they take good care to act
perfectly well as regards all district matters,
for most of the measures about which corrupt influences are at work relate to city affairs. The constituents of a country member know well how to judge him for those
of his acts which immediately affect themselves; but as regards others they often have
no means of forming an opinion, except
through the newspapers,—more especially
through the great metropolitan newspapers,
—and they have gradually come to look upon
all statements made by the latter with reference to the honesty or dishonesty of public
men with extreme distrust. This is because
our newspapers, including those who profes-
sedly stand as representatives of the highest
culture of the community, have been in the

habit of making such constant and reckless assaults upon the characters of even very good public men, as to greatly detract from their influence when they attack one who is really bad. They paint everyone with whom they disagree black. As a consequence the average man, who knows they are partly wrong, thinks they may also be partly right; he concludes that no man is absolutely white, and at the same time that no one is as black as he is painted; and takes refuge in the belief that all alike are gray. It then becomes impossible to rouse him to make an effort either for a good man or against a scoundrel. Nothing helps dishonest politicians as much as this feeling; and among the chief instruments in its production we must number certain of our newspapers who are loudest in asserting that they stand on the highest moral plane. As for the other newspapers, those of frankly " sensational " character, such as the two which at present claim to have the largest circulation in New York, there is small need to characterize them; they

form a very great promotive to public corruption and private vice, and are on the
whole the most potent of all the forces for
evil which are at work in the city.

PERILS OF LEGISLATIVE LIFE.

HOWEVER, there can be no question that a
great many men do deteriorate very much
morally when they go to Albany. The last
accusation most of us would think of bring-
ing against that dear, dull, old Dutch city is
that of being a fast place; and yet there are
plenty of members coming from out-of-the-
way villages or quiet country towns on whom
Albany has as bad an effect as Paris sometimes has on wealthy young Americans
from the great seaboard cities. Many men
go to the Legislature with the set purpose of
making money; but many others, who afterwards become bad, go there intending to do
good work. These latter may be well-meaning, weak young fellows of some shallow
brightness, who expect to make names for
themselves; perhaps they are young lawyers,
or real-estate brokers, or small shop-keepers;

they achieve but little success; they gradually become conscious that their business is broken up, and that they have not enough ability to warrant any expectation of their continuing in public life; some great temptation comes in their way (a corporation which expects to be relieved of perhaps a million dollars of taxes by the passage of a bill can afford to pay high for voters); they fall, and that is the end of them. Indeed, legislative life has temptations enough to make it unadvisable for any weak man, whether young or old, to enter it.

ALLIES OF VICIOUS LEGISLATORS.

THE array of vicious legislators is swelled by a number of men who really at bottom are not bad. Foremost among these are those most hopeless of beings who are handicapped by having some measure which they consider it absolutely necessary for the sake of their own future to "get through." One of these men will have a bill, for instance, appropriating a sum of money from the State Treasury to clear out a river, dam

the outlet of a lake, or drain a marsh; it may
be, although not usually so, proper enough in
itself, but it is drawn up primarily in the
interest of a certain set of his constituents
who have given him clearly to understand
that his continuance in their good graces depends upon his success in passing the bill.
He feels that he must get it through at all
hazards; the bad men find this out, and tell
him he must count on their opposition unless
he consents also to help their measures; he
resists at first but sooner or later yields;
and from that moment his fate is sealed,—
so far as his ability to do any work of general good is concerned.

A still larger number of men are good
enough in themselves, but are " owned " by
third parties. Usually the latter are politicians who have absolute control of the district machine, or who are, at least, of very
great importance in the political affairs of
their district. A curious fact is that they are
not invariably, though usually, of the same
party as the member; for in some places,

especially in the lower portions of the great
cities, politics become purely a business, and
in the squabbles for offices of emolument it
becomes important for a local leader to have
supporters among all the factions. When
one of these supporters is sent to a legislative body, he is allowed to act with the rest
of his party on what his chief regards as the
unimportant questions of party or public interest, but he has to come in to heel at once
when any matter arises touching the said
chief's power, pocket, or influence.

Other members will be controlled by some
wealthy private citizen who is not in politics,
but who has business interests likely to be
affected by legislation, and who is therefore,
willing to subscribe heavily to the campaign
expenses of an individual or of an association so as to insure the presence in Albany of
someone who will give him information and
assistance.

On one occasion there came before a committee of which I happened to be a member,
a perfectly proper bill in the interest of a

certain corporation; the majority of the committee, six in number, were thoroughly bad men, who opposed the measure with the hope of being paid to cease their opposition. When I consented to take charge of the bill, I had stipulated that not a penny should be paid to insure its passage. It therefore became necessary to see what pressure could be brought to bear on the recalcitrant members; and, accordingly, we had to find out who were the authors and sponsors of their political being. Three proved to be under the control of local statesmen of the same party as themselves, and of equally bad moral character; one was ruled by a politician of unsavory reputation from a different city; the fifth, a Democrat, was owned by a Republican Federal official; and the sixth by the president of a horse-car company. A couple of letters from these two magnates forced the last members mentioned to change front on the bill with surprising alacrity.

Nowadays, however, the greatest danger is that the member will be a servile tool of the " boss " or " machine " of his own party, in which case he can very rarely indeed be a good public servant.

There are two classes of cases in which corrupt members get money. One is when a wealthy corporation buys through some measure which will be of great benefit to itself, although, perhaps an injury to the public at large; the other is when a member introduces a bill hostile to some moneyed interest, with the expectation of being paid to let the matter drop. The latter, technically called a " strike," is much the most common; for, in spite of the outcry against them in legislative matters, corporations are more often sinned against than sinning. It is difficult, for reasons already given, in either case to convict the offending member, though we have very good laws against bribery. The reform has got to come from the people at large. It will be hard to make any very great improvement in the character of the legislators until respectable people become more fully awake to their duties, and

until the newspapers become more truthful
and less reckless in their statements.

It is not a pleasant task to have to draw
one side of legislative life in such dark
colors; but as the side exists, and as the dark
lines never can be rubbed out until we have
manfully acknowledged that they are there
and need rubbing out, it seems the falsest of
false delicacy to refrain from dwelling upon
them. But it would be most unjust to accept this partial truth as being the whole
truth. We blame the Legislature for many
evils, the ultimate cause for whose existence
is to be found in our own shortcomings.

THE OTHER SIDE OF THE PICTURE.

THERE is a much brighter side to the pic-
ture, and this is the larger side, too. It
would be impossible to get together a body
of more earnest, upright, and disinterested
men than the band of legislators, largely
young men, who during the past three years
have averted so much evil and accomplished
so much good at Albany. They were able,

at least partially, to put into actual practice
the theories that had long been taught by the
intellectual leaders of the country. And the
life of a legislator who is earnest in his efforts faithfully to perform his duty as a
public servant, is harassing and laborious to
the last degree. He is kept at work from
eight to fourteen hours a day; he is obliged
to incur the bitterest hostility of a body of
men as powerful as they are unscrupulous,
who are always on the watch to find out, or
to make out, anything in his private or his
public life which can be used against him;
and he has on his side either a but partially
roused public opinion, or else a public opinion roused, it is true, but only blindly conscious of the evil from which it suffers, and
alike ignorant and unwilling to avail itself of
the proper remedy.

This body of legislators, who, at any rate,
worked honestly for what they thought right,
were, as a whole, quite unselfish, and were
not treated particularly well by their constituents. Most of them soon got to realize

the fact that if they wished to enjoy their brief space of political life (and most though not all of them did enjoy it) they would have to make it a rule never to consider, in deciding how to vote upon any question, how their vote would affect their own political prospects. No man can do good service in the Legislature as long as he is worrying over the effect of his actions upon his own future. After having learned this, most of them got on very happily indeed. As a rule, and where no matter of vital principle is involved, a member is bound to represent the views of those who have elected him; but there are times when the voice of the people is anything but the voice of God, and then a conscientious man is equally bound to disregard it.

In the long run, and on the average, the public will usually do justice to its representatives; but it is a very rough, uneven, and long-delayed justice. That is, judging from what I have myself seen of the way in which members were treated by their con-

stituents, I should say that the chances of
an honest man being retained in public life
were about ten per cent. better than if he
were dishonest, other things being equal.
This is not a showing very creditable to us as
a people; and the explanation is to be found
in the shortcomings peculiar to the different
classes of our honest and respectable voters,
—shortcomings which may be briefly out-
lined.

SHORTCOMINGS OF THE PEOPLE WHO SHOULD TAKE PART IN POLITICAL WORK.

THE people of means in all great cities
have in times past shamefully neglected their
political duties, and have been contemptu-
ously disregarded by the professional politicians in consequence. A number of them
will get together in a large hall, will vocifer-
ously demand " reform," as if it were some
concrete substance which could be handed
out to them in slices, and will then disband
with a feeling of the most serene self-satis-
faction, and the belief that they have done
their entire duty as citizens and members of

the community. It is an actual fact that
four out of five of our wealthy and educated
men, of those who occupy what is called
good social position, are really ignorant of
the nature of a caucus or a primary meeting, and never attend either. Now, under
our form of government, no man can accomplish anything by himself; he must work
in combination with others; and the men of
whom we are speaking will never carry their
proper weight in the political affairs of the
country until they have formed themselves
into some organization, or else, which would
be better, have joined some of the organizations already existing. But there seems
often to be a certain lack of the robuster
virtues in our educated men, which makes
them shrink from the struggle and the inevitable contact with rough politicians (who
must often be rudely handled before they
can be forced to behave); while their lack
of familiarity with their surroundings causes
them to lack discrimination between the politicians who are decent, and those who are

not; for in their eyes the two classes both
equally unfamiliar, are distinguishable. Another reason why this class is not of more
consequence in politics, is that it is often
really out of sympathy—or, at least, its
more conspicuous members are—with the
feelings and interests of the great mass of
the American people; and it is a discreditable
fact that it is in this class that what has been
most aptly termed the " colonial " spirit still
survives. Until this survival of the spirit of
colonial dependence is dead, those in whom
it exists will serve chiefly as laughing-stocks
to the shrewd, humorous, and prejudiced
people who form nine tenths of our body-
politic, and whose chief characteristics are
their intensely American habits of thought,
and their surly intolerance of anything like
subservience to outside and foreign influences.

From different causes, the laboring
classes, even when thoroughly honest at
heart, often fail to appreciate honesty in their
representatives. They are frequently not

well informed in regard to the character of
the latter, and they are apt to be led aside
by the loud professions of the so-called labor
reformers, who are always promising to procure by legislation the advantages which can
only come to working men, or to any other
men, by their individual or united energy,
intelligence, and forethought. Very much has
been accomplished by legislation for laboring
men, by procuring mechanics' lien laws, factory laws, etc.; and hence it often comes
that they think legislation can accomplish all
things for them; and it is only natural, for
instance, that a certain proportion of their
number should adhere to the demagogue
who votes for a law to double the rate of
wages, rather than to the honest man who
opposes it. When people are struggling for
the necessaries of existence, and vaguely
feel, no matter how wrongly, that they are
also struggling against an unjustly ordered
system of life, it is hard to convince them of
the truth that an ounce of performance on
their own part is worth a ton of legislative

promises to change in some mysterious manner that life-system.

In the country districts justice to a member is somewhat more apt to be done. When, as is so often the case, it is not done, the cause is usually to be sought for in the numerous petty jealousies and local rivalries which are certain to exist in any small community whose interests are narrow and most of whose members are acquainted with each other; and besides this, our country vote is essentially a Bourbon or Tory vote, being very slow to receive new ideas, very tenacious of old ones, and hence inclined to look with suspicion upon any one who tries to shape his course according to some standard differing from that which is already in existence.

The actual work of procuring the passage of a bill through the Legislature is in itself far from slight. The hostility of the actively bad has to be discounted in advance, and the indifference of the passive majority, who are neither very good nor very bad, has to be overcome. This can usually be accomplished only by stirring up their constituencies; and so, besides the constant watchfulness over the course of the measure through both houses and the continual debating and parliamentary fencing which is necessary, it is also indispensable to get the people of districts not directly affected by the bill alive to its importance, so as to induce their representatives to vote for it. Thus, when the bill to establish a State Park at Niagara was on its passage, it was found that the great majority of the country members were opposed to it, fearing that it might conceal some land-jobbing scheme, and also fearing that their constituents, whose vice is not extravagance, would not countenance so great an expenditure of public money. It was of no use arguing with the members, and instead the country newspapers were flooded with letters, pamphlets were circulated, visits and personal appeals were made, until a sufficient number of these members changed front to enable us to get the lacking votes.

LIFE IN THE LEGISLATURE.

As already said, some of us who usually
acted together took a great deal of genuine
enjoyment out of our experience at Albany.
We liked the excitement and perpetual conflict, the necessity for putting forth all our
powers to reach our ends, and the feeling
that we were really being of some use in
the world; and if we were often both sad-
dened and angered by the viciousness and
ignorance of some of our colleagues, yet, in
return, the latter many times unwittingly
furnished us a good deal of amusement by
their preposterous actions and speeches.
Some of these are worth repeating, though
they can never, in repetition, seem what they
were when they occurred. The names and
circumstances, of course, have been so
changed as to prevent the possibility of the
real heroes of them being recognized. It
must be understood that they stand for the
exceptional and not the ordinary workings
of the average legislative intellect. I have
heard more sound sense than foolishness

talked in Albany, but to record the former would only bore the reader. And we must bear in mind that while the ignorance of some of our representatives warrants our saying that they should not be in the Legislature, it does not at all warrant our condemning the system of government which permits them to be sent there. There is no system so good that it has not some disadvantages. The only way to teach our foreign-born fellow-citizens how to govern themselves, is to give each the full rights possessed by other American citizens; and it is not to be wondered at if they at first show themselves unskilful in the exercise of these rights. It has been my experience moreover in the Legislature that when Hans or Paddy does turn out really well, there are very few native Americans indeed who do better. A very large number of the ablest and most disinterested and public-spirited citizens in New York are by birth Germans; and their names are towers of strength in the community. When I had to name a committee

which was to do the most difficult, dangerous, and important work that came before
the Legislature at all during my presence in
it, I chose three of my four colleagues from
among those of my fellow-legislators who
were Irish either by birth or descent. One
of the warmest and most disinterested
friends I have ever had or hope to have in
New York politics, is by birth an Irishman,
and is also as genuine and good an American citizen as is to be found within the
United States.

A good many of the Yankees in the house
would blunder time and again; but their
blunders were generally merely stupid and
not at all amusing, while, on the contrary,
the errors of those who were of Milesian ex-
traction always possessed a most refreshing
originality.

INCIDENTS OF LEGISLATIVE EXPERIENCE.

IN 1882 the Democrats in the house had
a clear majority, but were for a long time
unable to effect an organization, owing to a
faction-fight in their own ranks between the

Tammany and anti-Tammany members, each side claiming the lion's share of the spoils. After a good deal of bickering, the anti-Tammany men drew up a paper containing a series of propositions, and submitted it to their opponents, with the prefatory remark, in writing, that it was an *ultimatum*. The Tammany members were at once summoned to an indignation meeting, their feelings closely resembling those of the famous fish-wife who was called a parallelopipedon. None of them had any very accurate idea as to what the word *ultimatum* meant; but that it was intensely offensive, not to say abusive, in its nature, they did not question for a moment. It was felt that some equivalent and equally strong term by which to call Tammany's proposed counter-address must be found immediately; but, as the Latin vocabulary of the members was limited, it was some time before a suitable term was forthcoming. Finally, by a happy inspiration, some gentlemen of classical education remembered the phrase *ipse dixit;* it was at once felt to be the very phrase required by the peculiar exigencies of the case, and next day the reply appeared, setting forth with well-satisfied gravity that, in response to the County Democracy's "*ultimatum,*" Tammany herewith produced her "*ipse dixit.*"

Public servants of higher grade than aldermen or assemblymen sometimes give words a wider meaning than would be found in the dictionary. In many parts of the United States, owing to a curious series of historical associations (which, by the way, it would be interesting to trace), anything foreign and un-English is called "Dutch," and it was in this sense that a member of a recent Congress used the term when, in speaking in favor of a tariff on works of art, he told of the reluctance with which he saw the productions of native artists exposed to competition " with Dutch daubs from Italy "; a sentence pleasing alike from its alliteration and from its bold disregard of geographic trivialities.

Often an orator of this sort will have his attention attracted by some high-sounding word, which he has not before seen, and which he treasures up to use in his next rhetorical flight, without regard to the exact meaning. There was a laboring man's advocate in the last Legislature, one of whose efforts attracted a good deal of attention from his magnificent heedlessness of technical accuracy in the use of similes. He was speaking against the convict contract-labor system, and wound up an already sufficiently remarkable oration with the still more startling ending that the system " was a vital cobra which was swamping the lives of the laboring men." Now, he had evidently carefully put together the sentence beforehand, and the process of mental synthesis by which he built it up must have been curious. " Vital " was, of course, used merely as an adjective of intensity; he was a little uncertain in his ideas as to what a " cobra " was, but took it for granted that it was some terrible manifestation of nature, possibly hos-

tile to man, like a volcano, or a cyclone, or
Niagara, for instance; then " swamping "
was chosen as describing an operation very
likely to be performed by Niagara, or a
cyclone, or a cobra; and behold, the sentence
was complete.

Sometimes a common phrase will be given
a new meaning. Thus, the mass of legislation is strictly local in its character. Over
a thousand bills come up for consideration
in the course of a session, but a very few
of which affect the interests of the State
at large. The latter and the more important
private bills are, or ought to be, carefully
studied by each member; but it is a physical impossibility for any one man to examine
the countless local bills of small importance.
For these we have to trust to the member
for the district affected, and when one comes
up the response to any inquiry about it is
usually, " Oh, it's a local bill, affecting so-
and so's district; he is responsible for it."
By degrees, some of the members get to use
" local " in the sense of unimportant, and a

few of the assemblymen of doubtful honesty gradually come to regard it as meaning a bill of no pecuniary interest to themselves. There was a smug little rascal in one of the last legislatures, who might have come out of one of Lever's novels. He was undoubtedly a bad case, but had a genuine sense of humor, and his " bulls " made him the delight of the house. One day I came in late, just as a bill was being voted on, and meeting my friend, hailed him, " Hello, Pat, what's up? what's this they're voting on? " to which Pat replied, with contemptuous indifference to the subject, but with a sly twinkle in his eye, " Oh, some unimportant measure, sorr; some local bill or other—*a constitutional amendment!* "

The old Dublin Parliament never listened to a better specimen of a bull than was contained in the speech of a very genial and pleasant friend of mine, a really finished orator, who, in the excitement attendant upon receiving Governor Cleveland's message vetoing the five-cent-fare bill, uttered the following sentence: "Mr. Speaker, I recognize the hand that crops out in that veto; *I have heard it before!"*

One member rather astonished us one day day by his use of the word "shibboleth." He had evidently concluded that this was merely a more elegant synonym of the good old word shillalah, and in reproving a colleague for opposing a bill to increase the salaries of public laborers, he said, very impressively, "The throuble wid the young man is, that he uses the wurrd economy as a shibboleth, wherewith to strike the working man." Afterwards he changed the metaphor, and spoke of a number of us as using the word "reform" as a shibboleth, behind which to cloak our evil intentions.

A mixture of classical and constitutional misinformation was displayed a few sessions past in the State Assembly when I was a member of the Legislature. It was on the occasion of that annual nuisance, the debate upon the Catholic Protectory item of the Supply Bill. Every year some one who is desirous of bidding for the Catholic vote introduces this bill, which appropriates a sum of varying dimensions for the support of the Catholic Protectory, an excellent institution, but one which has no right whatever to come to the State for support; each year the insertion of the item is opposed by a small number of men, including the more liberal Catholics themselves, on proper grounds, and by a larger number from simple bigotry—a fact which was shown two years ago, when many of the most bitter opponents of this measure cheerfully supported a similar and equally objectionable one in aid of a Protestant institution. On the occasion referred to there were two assemblymen, both Celtic gentlemen, who were rivals for the leadership of the minority; one of them a stout, red-faced man, who may go by the name of the " Colonel," owing to his having seen service in the army; while the other was a dapper voluble fellow, who had at one time been a civil justice and was called the " Judge." Somebody was opposing the insertion of the item on the ground (perfectly just, by the way) that it was unconstitutional and he dwelt upon this objection at some length. The Judge, who knew nothing of the constitution, except that it was continually being quoted against all of his favorite projects, fidgeted about for some time, and at last jumped up to know if he might ask the gentleman a question. The latter said, " Yes," and the Judge went on, " I'd like to know if the gintleman has ever personally seen the Catholic Protectoree? " " No, I haven't," said his astonished opponent. " Then, phwat do you mane by talking about its being unconstitootional? It's no more unconstitootional than you are! " Then, turning to the house, with slow and withering sarcasm, he added, " The throuble wid the gintleman is that he okkipies what lawyers would call a kind of a quasi-position upon this bill," and sat down amid the applause of his followers.

His rival, the Colonel, felt he had gained altogether too much glory from the en-

counter, and after the nonplussed country-
man had taken his seat, he stalked solemnly
over to the desk of the elated Judge, looked
at him majestically for a moment, and said,
" You'll excuse my mentioning, sorr, that
the gintleman who has just sat down knows
more law in a wake than you do in a month;
and more than that, Mike Shaunnessy, phwat
do you mane by quotin' Latin on the flure
of this House, *when you don't know the alpha
and omayga of the language!*" and back he
walked, leaving the Judge in humiliated sub-
mission behind him.

The Judge was always falling foul of the
Constitution. Once, when defending one of
his bills which made a small but wholly in-
defensible appropriation of State money for
a private purpose, he asserted " that the Constitution didn't touch little things like that ";
and on another occasion he remarked to me
that he " never allowed the Constitution to
come between friends."

The Colonel was at that time chairman of
a committee, before which there sometimes

came questions affecting the interests or supposed interests of labor. The committee
was hopelessly bad in its composition, most
of the members being either very corrupt or
exceedingly inefficient. The Colonel generally kept order with a good deal of dignity;
indeed, when, as not infrequently happened,
he had looked upon the rye that was flavored
with lemon-peel, his sense of personal dignity grew till it became fairly majestic, and
he ruled the committee with a rod of iron.
At one time a bill had been introduced (one of
the several score of preposterous measures
that annually make their appearance purely for
purposes of buncombe), by whose terms all
laborers in the public works of great cities
were to receive three dollars a day—double
the market price of labor. To this bill, by
the way, an amendment was afterwards offered in the house by some gentleman with
a sense of humor, which was to make it read
that all the inhabitants of great cities were
to receive three dollars a day, and the privilege of laboring on the public works if they

chose; the original author of the bill questioning doubtfully if the amendment " didn't make the measure too sweeping." The measure was, of course, of no consequence whatever to the genuine laboring men, but was of interest to the professional labor agitators; and a body of the latter requested leave to appear before the committee. This was granted, but on the appointed day the chairman turned up in a condition of such portentous dignity as to make it evident that he had been on a spree of protracted duration. Down he sat at the head of the table, and glared at the committeemen, while the latter, whose faces would not have looked amiss in a rogues' gallery, cowered before him. The first speaker was a typical professional laboring man; a sleek, oily little fellow, with a black mustache, who had never done a stroke of work in his life. He felt confident that the Colonel would favor him, —a confidence soon to be rudely shaken,— and began with a deprecatory smile:

" Humble though I am——"

Rap, rap, went the chairman's gavel, and the following dialogue occurred:

Chairman (with dignity). "What's that you said you were, sir?"

Professional Workingman (decidedly taken aback). "I—I said I was humble, sir?"

Chairman (reproachfully). "Are you an American citizen, sir?"

P. W. "Yes, sir."

Chairman (with emphasis). "Then you're the equal of any man in this State! Then you're the equal of any man on this committee! *Don't let me hear you call yourself humble again! Go on sir!*"

After this warning the advocate managed to keep clear of the rocks until, having worked himself up to quite a pitch of excitement, he incautiously exclaimed, "But the poor man has no friends!" which brought the Colonel down on him at once. Rap, rap, went his gavel, and he scowled grimly at the offender while he asked with deadly deliberation:

"What did you say that time, sir?"

P. W. (hopelessly). "I said the poor man had no friends, sir."

Chairman (with sudden fire). "Then you lied, sir! I am the poor man's friend! so are my colleagues, sir!" (Here the rogues' gallery tried to look benevolent.) "Speak the truth, sir!" (with sudden change from the manner admonitory to the manner mandatory). "Now, you sit down quick, or get out of this somehow!"

This put an end to the sleek gentleman, and his place was taken by a fellow-professional of another type—a great, burly man, who would talk to you on private matters in a perfectly natural tone of voice, but who, the minute he began to speak of the Wrongs (with a capital W) of Labor (with a capital L), bellowed as if he had been a bull of Bashan. The Colonel, by this time pretty far gone, eyed him malevolently, swaying to and fro in his chair. However, the first effect of the fellow's oratory was soothing rather than otherwise, and produced the un-

expected result of sending the chairman fast
asleep sitting bolt upright. But in a minute or two, as the man warmed up to his
work, he gave a peculiarly resonant howl
which waked the Colonel up. The latter
came to himself with a jerk, looked fixedly
at the audience, caught sight of the speaker,
remembered having seen him before, forgot
that he had been asleep, and concluded that
it must have been on some previous day.
Hammer, hammer, went the gavel, and—

"I've seen you before, sir!"

"You have not," said the man.

"Don't tell me I lie, sir!" responded the
Colonel, with sudden ferocity. "You've
addressed this committee on a previous
day!"

"I've never—" began the man; but the
Colonel broke in again:

"Sit down, sir! The dignity of the chair
must be preserved! No man shall speak to
this committee twice. The committee stands
adjourned." And with that he stalked majestically out of the room, leaving the com-

mittee and the delegation to gaze sheepishly into each other's faces.

OUTSIDERS.

AFTER all, outsiders furnish quite as much fun as the legislators themselves. The number of men who persist in writing one letters of praise, abuse, and advice on every conceivable subject is appalling; and the writers are of every grade, from the lunatic and the criminal up. The most difficult to deal with are the men with hobbies. There is the Protestant fool, who thinks that our liberties are menaced by the machinations of the Church of Rome; and his companion idiot, who wants legislation against all secret societies, especially the Masons. Then there are the believers in " isms " of whom the women-suffragists stand in the first rank. Now I have always been a believer in woman's rights, but I must confess I have never seen such a hopelessly impracticable set of persons as the woman-suffragists who came up to Albany to get legislation. They simply would not draw up their measures in proper form; when I pointed out to one of them that their proposed bill was drawn up in direct defiance of certain of the sections of the Constitution of the State he blandly replied that he did not care at all for that, because the measure had been drawn up so as to be in accord with the Constitution of Heaven. There was no answer to this beyond the very obvious one that Albany was in no way akin to Heaven. The ultra-temperance people—not the moderate and sensible ones—are quite as impervious to common sense.

A member's correspondence is sometimes amusing. A member receives shoals of letters of advice, congratulation, entreaty, and abuse, half of them anonymous. Most of these are stupid; but some are at least out of the common.

I had some constant correspondents. One lady in the western part of the State wrote me a weekly disquisition on woman's rights. A Buffalo clergyman spent two years on a one-sided correspondence about prohibition. A gentleman of Syracuse wrote me such a stream of essays and requests about the charter of that city that I feared he would drive me into a lunatic asylum; but he anticipated matters by going into one himself. A New Yorker at regular intervals sent up a request that I would " reintroduce " the Dongan charter, which had lapsed two centuries before. A gentleman interested in a proposed law to protect primaries took to telegraphing daily questions as to its progress—a habit of which I broke him by sending in response telegrams of several hundred words each, which I was careful not to prepay.

There are certain legislative actions which must be taken in a purely Pickwickian sense. Notable among these are the resolutions of sympathy for the alleged oppressed patriots and peoples of Europe. These are generally directed against England, as there exists in the lower strata of political life an Anglophobia quite as objectionable as the Anglomania of the higher social circles.

As a rule, these resolutions are to be classed as simply *bouffe* affairs; they are commonly introduced by some ambitious legislator—often, I regret to say, a native American—who has a large foreign vote in his district. During my term of service in the Legislature, resolutions were introduced demanding the recall of Minister Lowell, assailing the Czar for his conduct towards the Russian Jews, sympathizing with the Land League and the Dutch Boers, etc., etc.; the passage of each of which we strenuously and usually successfully opposed, on the ground that while we would warmly welcome any foreigner who came here, and in good faith assumed the duties of American citizenship, we had a right to demand in return that he should not bring any of his race or national antipathies into American political life. Resolutions of this character are sometimes undoubtedly proper; but in nine cases out of ten they are wholly unjustifiable. An instance of this sort of thing which took place not at Albany may be cited. Recently the Board of Aldermen of one of our great cities received a stinging rebuke, which it is to be feared the aldermanic intellect was too dense fully to appreciate. The aldermen passed a resolution " condemning " the Czar of Russia for his conduct towards his fellow-citizens of Hebrew faith, and " demanding " that he should forthwith treat them better; this was forwarded to the Russian Minister, with a request that it be sent to the Czar. It came back forty-eight hours afterwards, with a note on the back by one of the under-secretaries of the legation, to the effect that as he was not aware that Russia had any diplomatic relations with this particular Board of Aldermen, and as, indeed, Russia was not officially cognizant of their existence, and, moreover, was wholly indifferent to their opinions on any conceivable subject, he herewith returned them their kind communication.[1]

[1] A few years later a member of the Italian Legation "scored" heavily on one of our least pleasant national peculiarities. An Italian had just been

In concluding I would say, that while there is so much evil at Albany, and so much reason for our exerting ourselves to bring about a better state of things, yet there is no cause for being disheartened or for thinking that it is hopeless to expect improvement. On the contrary, the standard of legislative morals is certainly higher than it was fifteen years ago or twenty-five years ago. In the future it may either improve or retrograde, by fits and starts, for it will keep pace exactly with the awakening of the popular mind to the necessity of having honest and intelligent representatives in the State Legislature.[1]

lynched in Colorado, and an Italian paper in New York bitterly denounced the Italian Minister for his supposed apathy in the matter. The member of the Legation in question answered that the accusations were most unjust, for the Minister had worked zealously until he found that the deceased "had taken out his naturalization papers, and was entitled to all the privileges of American citizenship."

[1] At present, twelve years later, I should say that there was rather less personal corruption in the Legislature; but also less independence and

I have had opportunity of knowing something about the workings of but a few of our other State legislatures: from what I have seen and heard, I should say that we stand about on a par with those of Pennsylvania, Maryland, and Illinois, above that of Louisiana, and below those of Vermont, Massachusetts, Rhode Island, and Wyoming, as well as below the national legislature at Washington. But the moral status of a legislative body, especially in the West, often varies widely from year to year.

greater subservience to the machine, which is even less responsive to honest and enlightened public opinion.

VI

MACHINE POLITICS IN NEW YORK CITY [1]

IN New York city, as in most of our other great municipalities, the direction of political affairs has been for many years mainly in the hands of a class of men who make politics their regular business and means of livelihood. These men are able to keep their grip only by means of the singularly perfect way in which they have succeeded in organizing their respective parties and factions; and it is in consequence of the clock-work regularity and efficiency with which these several organizations play their parts, alike for good and for evil, that they have been nicknamed by outsiders "machines," while the men who take part in and control, or, as they would themselves say,

[1] The *Century*, November, 1886.

" run " them, now form a well-recognized and fairly well-defined class in the community, and are familiarly known as machine politicians. It may be of interest to sketch in outline some of the characteristics of these men and of their machines, the methods by which and the objects for which they work, and the reasons for their success in the political field.

The terms machine and machine politician are now undoubtedly used ordinarily in a reproachful sense; but it does not at all follow that this sense is always the right one. On the contrary, the machine is often a very powerful instrument for good; and a machine politician really desirous of doing honest work on behalf of the community, is fifty times as useful an ally as is the average philanthropic outsider. Indeed, it is of course true, that any political organization (and absolutely no good work can be done in politics without an organization) is a machine; and any man who perfects and uses this organization is himself, to a certain extent, a machine politician. In the rough, however, the feeling against machine politics and politicians is tolerably well justified by the facts, although this statement really reflects most severely upon the educated and honest people who largely hold themselves aloof from public life, and show a curious incapacity for fulfilling their public duties.

The organizations that are commonly and distinctively known as machines are those belonging to the two great recognized parties, or to their factional subdivisions; and the reason why the word machine has come to be used, to a certain extent, as a term of opprobrium is to be found in the fact that these organizations are now run by the leaders very largely as business concerns to benefit themselves and their followers, with little regard to the community at large. This is natural enough. The men having control and doing all the work have gradually come to have the same feeling about politics that other men have about the business of a merchant or manufacturer; it was too much to expect that if left entirely to themselves they would continue disinterestedly to work for the benefit of others. Many a machine politician who is to-day a most unwholesome influence in our politics is in private life quite as respectable as anyone else; only he has forgotten that his business affects the state at large, and, regarding it as merely his own private concern, he has carried into it the same selfish spirit that actuates in business matters the majority of the average mercantile community. A merchant or manufacturer works his business, as a rule, purely for his own benefit, without any regard whatever for the community at large. The merchant uses all his influence for a low tariff, and the manufacturer is even more strenuously in favor of protection, not at all from any theory of abstract right, but because of self-interest. Each views such a political question as the tariff, not from the standpoint of how it will affect the nation as a whole, but merely from that of how it will affect him personally. If a community were

in favor of protection, but nevertheless per-
mitted all the governmental machinery to fall
into the hands of importing merchants, it
would be small cause for wonder if the latter shaped the laws to suit themselves, and
the chief blame, after all, would rest with
the supine and lethargic majority which
failed to have enough energy to take charge
of their own affairs. Our machine politicians, in actual life act in just this same way;
their actions are very often dictated by selfish motives, with but little regard for the
people at large though, like the merchants,
they often hold a very high standard of honor
on certain points; they therefore need continually to be watched and opposed by those
who wish to see good government. But,
after all, it is hardly to be wondered at that
they abuse power which is allowed to fall into
their hands owing to the ignorance or timid
indifference of those who by rights should
themselves keep it.

In a society properly constituted for true
democratic government—in a society such

as that seen in many of our country towns, for example—machine rule is impossible. But in New York, as well as in most of our other great cities, the conditions favor the growth of ring or boss rule. The chief causes thus operating against good government are the moral and mental attitudes towards politics assumed by different sections of the voters. A large number of these are simply densely ignorant, and, of course, such are apt to fall under the influence of cunning leaders, and even if they do right, it is by hazard merely. The criminal class in a great city is always of some size, while what may be called the potentially criminal class is still larger. Then there is a great class of laboring men, mostly of foreign birth or parentage, who at present both expect too much from legislation and yet at the same time realize too little how powerfully though indirectly they are affected by a bad or corrupt government. In many wards the overwhelming majority of the voters do not realize that heavy taxes fall ultimately upon them, and actually view with perfect complacency burdens laid by their representatives upon the tax-payers, and, if anything, approve of a hostile attitude towards the latter—having a vague feeling of animosity towards them as possessing more than their proper proportion of the world's good things, and sharing with most other human beings the capacity to bear with philosophic equanimity ills merely affecting one's neighbors. When powerfully roused on some financial, but still more on some sentimental question, this same laboring class will throw its enormous and usually decisive weight into the scale which it believes inclines to the right; but its members are often curiously and cynically indifferent to charges of corruption against favorite heroes or demagogues, so long as these charges do not imply betrayal of their own real or fancied interests. Thus an alderman or assemblyman representing certain wards may make as much money as he pleases out of corporations without seriously jeopardizing his standing with his constituents; but if he once, whether from honest or dishonest motives, stands by a corporation when the interests of the latter are supposed to conflict with those of "the people," it is all up with him. These voters are, moreover, very emotional; they value in a public man what we are accustomed to consider virtues only to be taken into account when estimating private character. Thus, if a man is open-handed and warm-hearted, they consider it as a fair offset to his being a little bit shaky when it comes to applying the eighth commandment to affairs of state. I have more than once heard the statement, "He is very liberal to the poor," advanced as a perfectly satisfactory answer to the charge that a certain public man was corrupt. Moreover, working men, whose lives are passed in one unceasing round of narrow and monotonous toil, are not unnaturally inclined to pay heed to the demagogues and professional labor advocates who promise if elected to try to pass laws to better their condition;

they are hardly prepared to understand or
approve the American doctrine of government, which is that the state cannot ordinarily attempt to better the condition of a
man or a set of men, but can merely see that
no wrong is done him or them by anyone
else, and that all alike have a fair chance in
the struggle for life—a struggle wherein, it
may as well at once be freely though sadly
acknowedged, very many are bound to fail,
no matter how ideally perfect any given system of government may be.

Of course it must be remembered that all
these general statements are subject to an
immense number of individual exceptions;
there are tens of thousands of men who work
with their hands for their daily bread and yet
put into actual practice that sublime virtue
of disinterested adherence to the right, even
when it seems likely merely to benefit others,
and those others better off than they themselves are; for they vote for honesty and
cleanliness, in spite of great temptation to do

the opposite, and in spite of their not seeing how any immediate benefit will result to themselves.

REASONS FOR THE NEGLECT OF PUBLIC DUTIES BY RESPECTABLE MEN IN EASY CIRCUMSTANCES.

THIS class is composed of the great bulk of the men who range from well-to-do up to very rich; and of these the former generally and the latter almost universally neglect their political duties, for the most part rather pluming themselves upon their good conduct if they so much as vote on election day. This largely comes from the tremendous wear and tension of life in our great cities. Moreover, the men of small means with us are usually men of domestic habits; and this very devotion to home, which is one of their chief virtues, leads them to neglect their public duties. They work hard, as clerks, mechanics, small tradesmen, etc., all day long, and when they get home in the evening they dislike to go out. If they do go to a ward meeting they find themselves isolated, and strangers both to the men whom they meet and to the matter on which they have to act; for in the city a man is quite as sure to know next to nothing about his neighbors as in the country he is to be intimately acquainted with them. In the country the people of a neighborhood, when they assemble in one of their local conventions, are already well acquainted, and therefore able to act together with effect; whereas in the city, even if the ordinary citizens do come out, they are totally unacquainted with one another, and are as helplessly unable to oppose the disciplined ranks of the professional politicians as is the case with a mob of freshmen in one of our colleges when in danger of being hazed by the sophomores. Moreover, the pressure of competition in city life is so keen that men often have as much as they can do to attend to their own affairs, and really hardly have the leisure to look after those of the public. The general tendency everywhere is toward the specialization of functions, and this holds good as well in politics as elsewhere.

The reputable private citizens of small means thus often neglect to attend to their public duties because to do so would perhaps interfere with their private business. This is bad enough, but the case is worse with the really wealthy, who still more generally neglect these same duties, partly because not to do so would interfere with their pleasure, and partly from a combination of other motives, all of them natural but none of them creditible. A successful merchant, well dressed, pompous, self-important, un-used to any life outside of the counting-room, and accustomed because of his very success to be treated with deferential regard, as one who stands above the common run of humanity, naturally finds it very unpleasant to go to a caucus or primary where he has to stand on an equal footing with his groom and day-laborers, and indeed may discover that the latter, thanks to their faculty for combination, are rated higher in the scale of

political importance than he is himself. In
all the large cities of the North the wealthier,
or, as they would prefer to style themselves,
the " upper " classes, tend distinctly towards
the bourgeois type; and an individual in the
bourgeois stage of development, while
honest, industrious, and virtuous, is also not
unapt to be a miracle of timid and short-
sighted selfishness. The commercial classes
are only too likely to regard everything
merely from the standpoint of " Does it
pay? " and many a merchant does not take
any part in politics because he is short-
sighted enough to think that it will pay him
better to attend purely to making money,
and too selfish to be willing to undergo any
trouble for the sake of abstract duty; while
the younger men of this type are too much
engrossed in their various social pleasures
to be willing to give their time to anything
else. It is also unfortunately true, especially
throughout New England and the Middle
States, that the general tendency among
people of culture and high education has

been to neglect and even to look down upon
the rougher and manlier virtues, so that an
advanced state of intellectual development
is too often associated with a certain effem-
inacy of character. Our more intellectual
men often shrink from the raw coarseness
and the eager struggle of political life as if
they were women. Now, however refined
and virtuous a man may be, he is yet entirely out of place in the American body-
politic unless he is himself of sufficiently
coarse fibre and virile character to be more
angered than hurt by an insult or injury;
the timid good form a most useless as well
as a most despicable portion of the community. Again, when a man is heard objecting to taking part in politics because it
is "low," he may be set down as either a
fool or a coward: it would be quite as sensible for a militiaman to advance the same
statement as an excuse for refusing to assist
in quelling a riot. Many cultured men neglect their political duties simply because
they are too delicate to have the element of

" strike back " in their natures, and because
they have an unmanly fear of being forced
to stand up for their own rights when
threatened with abuse or insult. Such are
the conditions which give the machine men
their chance; and they have been able to
make the most possible out of this chance,—
first, because of the perfection to which they
have brought their machinery, and, second,
because of the social character of their political organizations.

ORGANIZATION AND WORK OF THE MACHINES.

THE machinery of any one of our political
bodies is always rather complicated; and its
politicians invariably endeavor to keep it so,
because, their time being wholly given to it,
they are able to become perfectly familiar
with all its workings, while the average outsider becomes more and more helpless in
proportion as the organization is less and
less simple. Besides some others of minor
importance, there are at present in New

York three great political organizations, *viz.,*
those of the regular Republicans, of the
County Democracy,[1] and of Tammany Hall,
that of the last being perhaps the most perfect, viewed from a machine standpoint.
Although with wide differences in detail, all
these bodies are organized upon much the
same general plan; and one description may
be taken in the rough, as applying to all.
There is a large central committee, composed
of numerous delegates from the different assembly districts, which decides upon the
various questions affecting the party as a
whole in the county and city; and then there
are the various organizations in the assembly
districts themselves, which are the real
sources of strength, and with which alone
it is necessary to deal. There are different
rules for the admission to the various district primaries and caucuses of the voters
belonging to the respective parties; but in
almost every case the real work is done and

[1] Since succeeded every year or two by some
other anti-Tammany Democratic organization or
organizations.

the real power held by a small knot of men, who in turn pay a greater or less degree of fealty to a single boss.

The mere work to be done on election day and in preparing for it forms no slight task. There is an association in each assembly or election district, with its president, secretary, treasurer, executive committee, etc.; these call the primaries and caucuses, arrange the lists of the delegates to the various nominating conventions, raise funds for campaign purposes, and hold themselves in communication with their central party organizations. At the primaries in each assembly district a full set of delegates is chosen to nominate assemblymen and aldermen, while others are chosen to go to the State, county, and congressional conventions. Before election day many thousands of complete sets of the party ticket are printed, folded, and put together, or, as it is called, "bunched." A single bundle of these ballots is then sent to every voter in the district, while thousands are reserved for distribution at the polls. In every election precinct—there are probably twenty or thirty in each assembly district—a captain and from two to a dozen subordinates are appointed.[1] These have charge of the actual giving out of the ballots at the polls. On election day they are at their places long before the hour set for voting; each party has a wooden booth, looking a good deal like a sentry-box, covered over with flaming posters containing the names of their nominees, and the "workers" cluster around these as centres. Every voter as he approaches is certain to be offered a set of tickets; usually these sets are "straight," that is, contain all the nominees of one party, but frequently crooked work will be done, and some one candidate will get his own ballots bunched with the rest of those of the opposite party. Each captain of a district is generally paid a certain sum of money, greater or less according to his ability as a

[1] All this has been changed, vastly for the better, by the ballot reform laws, under which the State distributes the printed ballots; and elections are now much more honest than formerly.

politician or according to his power of serving the boss or machine. Nominally this money goes in paying the subordinates and in what are vaguely termed " campaign expenses," but as a matter of fact it is in many instances simply pocketed by the recipient; indeed, very little of the large sums of money annually spent by candidates to bribe voters actually reaches the voters supposed to be bribed. The money thus furnished is procured either by subscriptions from rich outsiders, or by assessments upon the candidates themselves; formerly much was also obtained from office-holders, but this is now prohibited by law. A great deal of money is also spent in advertising, placarding posters, paying for public meetings, and organizing and uniforming members to take part in some huge torchlight procession— this last particular form of spectacular enjoyment being one peculiarly dear to the average American political mind. Candidates for very lucrative positions are often assessed really huge sums, in order to pay for the extravagant methods by which our canvasses are conducted. Before a legislative committee of which I was a member, the Register of New York County blandly testified under oath that he had forgotten whether his expenses during his canvass had been over or under fifty thousand dollars. It must be remembered that even now—and until recently the evil was very much greater —the rewards paid to certain public officials are out of all proportion to the services rendered; and in such cases the active managing politicians feel that they have a right to exact the heaviest possible toll from the candidate, to help pay the army of hungry heelers who do their bidding. Thus, before the same committee the County Clerk testified that his income was very nearly eighty thousand a year, but with refreshing frankness admitted that his own position was practically merely that of a figure-head, and that all the work was done by his deputy, on a small fixed salary. As the County Clerk's term is three years, he should nominally

have received nearly a quarter of a million
dollars; but as a matter of fact two thirds
of the money went to the political organizations with which he was connected. The
enormous emoluments of such officers are,
of course, most effective in debauching
politics. They bear no relation whatever
to the trifling quantity of work done, and
the chosen candidate readily recognizes
what is the exact truth,—namely, that the
benefit of his service is expected to enure
to his party allies, and not to the citizens
at large. Thus, one of the county officers
who came before the above-mentioned committee, testified with a naïve openness
which was appalling, in answer to what was
believed to be a purely formal question as to
whether he performed his public duties
faithfully, that he did so perform them whenever they did not conflict with his political
duties!—meaning thereby, as he explained,
attending to his local organizations, seeing
politicians, fixing primaries, bailing out those
of his friends (apparently by no means few

in number) who got hauled up before a justice of the peace, etc., etc.   This man's statements were valuable because, being a truthful person and of such dense ignorance that
he was at first wholly unaware his testimony
was in any way remarkable, he really tried to
tell things as they were; and it had evidently
never occurred to him that he was not expected by everyone to do just as he had been
doing,—that is, to draw a large salary for
himself, to turn over a still larger fund to his
party allies, and conscientiously to endeavor,
as far as he could, by the free use of his time
and influence, to satisfy the innumerable de-
mands made upon him by the various small-
fry politicians.[1]

" HEELERS."

THE " heelers," or " workers," who stand
at the polls, and are paid in the way above
described, form a large part of the rank and

[1] As a consequence of our investigation the committee, of which I was chairman, succeeded in
securing the enactment of laws which abolished
these enormous salaries.

file composing each organization. There are, of course, scores of them in each assembly district association, and, together with the almost equally numerous class of federal, State, or local paid officeholders (except in so far as these last have been cut out by the operations of the civil-service reform laws), they form the bulk of the men by whom the machine is run, the bosses of great and small degree chiefly merely oversee the work and supervise the deeds of their henchmen. The organization of a party in our city is really much like that of an army. There is one great central boss, assisted by some trusted and able lieutenants; these communicate with the different district bosses, whom they alternately bully and assist. The district boss in turn has a number of half-subordinates, half-allies, under him; these latter choose the captains of the election districts, etc., and come into contact wth the common heelers. The more stupid and ignorant the common heelers are, and the more implicitly they obey orders, the greater becomes the effectiveness of the machine. An ideal machine has for its officers men of marked force, cunning and unscrupulous, and for its common soldiers men who may be either corrupt or moderately honest, but who must be of low intelligence. This is the reason why such a large proportion of the members of every political machine are recruited from the lower grades of the foreign population. These henchmen obey unhesitatingly the orders of their chiefs, both at the primary or caucus and on election day, receiving regular rewards for so doing, either in employment procured for them or else in money outright. Of course it is by no means true that these men are all actuated merely by mercenary motives. The great majority entertain also a real feeling of allegiance towards the party to which they belong, or towards the political chief whose fortunes they follow; and many work entirely without pay and purely for what they believe to be right. Indeed, an experienced politician always greatly prefers to have under him men whose hearts are in their work and upon whose unbribed devotion he can rely; but unfortunately he finds in most cases that their exertions have to be seconded by others which are prompted by motives far more mixed.

All of these men, whether paid or not, make a business of political life and are thoroughly at home among the obscure intrigues that go to make up so much of it; and consequently they have quite as much the advantage when pitted against amateurs as regular soldiers have when matched against militiamen. But their numbers, though absolutely large, are, relatively to the entire community, so small that some other cause must be taken into consideration in order to account for the commanding position occupied by the machine and the machine politicians in public life. This other determining cause is to be found in the fact that all these machine associations have a

social as well as a political side, and that a
large part of the political life of every leader
or boss is also identical with his social life.

THE SOCIAL SIDE OF MACHINE POLITICS.

THE political associations of the various
districts are not organized merely at the approach of election day; on the contrary, they
exist throughout the year, and for the
greater part of the time are to a great extent merely social clubs. To a large number
of the men who belong to them they are
the chief social rallying-point. These men
congregate in the association building in the
evening to smoke, drink beer, and play cards,
precisely as the wealthier men gather in the
clubs whose purpose is avowedly social and
not political—such as the Union, University,
and Knickerbocker. Politics thus becomes
a pleasure and relaxation as well as a serious
pursuit. The different members of the same
club or association become closely allied with
one another, and able to act together on occasions with unison and *esprit de corps;* and

they will stand by one of their own number
for reasons precisely homologous to those
which make a member of one of the upper
clubs support a fellow-member if the latter
happens to run for office. " He is a gentleman, and shall have my vote," says the swell
club man. " He's one of the boys, and I'm
for him," replies the heeler from the district
party association. In each case the feeling
is social rather than political, but where the
club man influences one vote the heeler controls ten. A rich merchant and a small
tradesman alike find it merely a bore to attend the meetings of the local political club;
it is to them an irksome duty which is
shirked whenever possible. But to the small
politicians and to the various workers and
hangers-on, these meetings have a distinct
social attraction, and the attendance is a
matter of preference. They are in congenial
society and in the place where by choice they
spend their evenings, and where they bring
their friends and associates; and naturally
all the men so brought together gradually

blend their social and political ties, and work
with an effectiveness impossible to the outside citizens whose social instincts interfere,
instead of coinciding with their political
duties. If an ordinary citizen wishes to have
a game of cards or a talk with some of his
companions, he must keep away from the
local headquarters of his party; whereas,
under similar circumstances, the professional
politician must go there. The man who is
fond of his home naturally prefers to stay
there in the evening, rather than go out
among the noisy club frequenters, whose
pleasure it is to see each other at least
weekly, and who spend their evenings discussing neither sport, business, nor scandal,
as do other sections of the community, but
the equally monotonous subject of ward
politics.

The strength of our political organizations
arises from their development as social
bodies; many of the hardest workers in their
ranks are neither office-holders nor yet paid
henchmen, but merely members who have

gradually learned to identify their fortunes with the party whose hall they have come to regard as the head-quarters in which to spend the most agreeable of their leisure moments. Under the American system it is impossible for a man to accomplish anything by himself; he must associate himself with others, and they must throw their weight together. This is just what the social functions of the political clubs enable their members to do. The great and rich society clubs are composed of men who are not apt to take much interest in politics anyhow, and never act as a body. The great effect produced by a social organization for political purposes is shown by the career of the Union League Club; and equally striking proof can be seen by every man who attends a ward meeting. There is thus, however much to be regretted it may be, a constant tendency towards the concentration of political power in the hands of those men who by taste and education are fitted to enjoy the social side of the various political organizations.

THE LIQUOR-SELLER IN POLITICS.

IT is this that gives the liquor-sellers their enormous influence in politics. Preparatory to the general election of 1884, there were held in the various districts of New York ten hundred and seven primaries and political conventions of all parties, and of these no less than six hundred and thirty-three took place in liquor-saloons,—a showing that leaves small ground for wonder at the low average grade of the nominees. The reason for such a condition of things is perfectly evident: it is because the liquor-saloons are places of social resort for the same men who turn the local political organizations into social clubs. Bar-tenders form perhaps the nearest approach to a leisure class that we have at present on this side of the water. Naturally they are on semi-intimate terms with all who frequent their houses. There is no place where more gossip is talked than in bar-rooms, and much of this gossip is about politics,—that is, the politics of the ward, not of the nation. The tariff and the silver question may be alluded to and civil-service reform may be incidentally damned, but the real interest comes in discussing the doings of the men with whom they are personally acquainted: why Billy so-and-so, the alderman, has quarrelled with his former chief supporter; whether " old man X " has really managed to fix the delegates to a given convention; the reason why one faction bolted at the last primary; and if it is true that a great down-town boss who has an intimate friend of opposite political faith running in an up-town district has forced the managers of his own party to put up a man of straw against him. The bar-keeper is a man of much local power, and is, of course, hail-fellow-well-met with his visitors, as he and they can be of mutual assistance to one another. Even if of different politics, their feelings towards each other are influenced purely by personal considerations; and, in-deed, this is true of most of the smaller bosses as regards their dealings among

themselves, for, as one of them once remarked to me with enigmatic truthfulness,
"there are no politics in politics" of the
lower sort—which, being interpreted, means
that a professional politician is much less
apt to be swayed by the fact of a man's being a Democrat or a Republican than he is
by his being a personal friend or foe. The
liquor-saloons thus become the social head-
quarters of the little knots or cliques of men
who take most interest in local political affairs; and by an easy transition they become
the political head-quarters when the time for
preparing for the elections arrives; and, of
course, the good-will of the owners of the
places is thereby propitiated,—an important
point with men striving to control every vote
possible.

The local political clubs also become to a
certain extent mutual benefit associations.
The men in them become pretty intimate
with one another; and in the event of one
becoming ill, or from any other cause thrown
out of employment, his fellow-members will

very often combine to assist him through his troubles, and quite large sums are frequently raised for such a purpose. Of course, this forms an additional bond among the members, who become closely knit together by ties of companionship, self-interest, and mutual interdependence. Very many members of these associations come into them without any thought of advancing their own fortunes; they work very hard for their party, or rather for the local body bearing the party name, but they do it quite disinterestedly, and from a feeling akin to that which we often see make other men devote their time and money to advancing the interests of a yacht club or racing stable, although no immediate benefit can result therefrom to themselves. One such man I now call to mind who is by no means well off, and is neither an office-seeker nor an office-holder, but who regularly every year spends about fifty dollars at election time for the success of the party, or rather the wing of the party, to which he belongs. He has a personal

pride in seeing his pet candidates rolling up
large majorities. Men of this stamp also
naturally feel most enthusiasm for, or animosity against, the minor candidates with
whom they are themselves acquainted. The
names at the head of the ticket do not, to
their minds, stand out with much individuality; and while such names usually command the normal party support, yet very
often there is an infinitely keener rivalry
among the smaller politicians over candidates for local offices. I remember, in 1880,
a very ardent Democratic ward club, many
of the members of which in the heat of a
contest for an assemblyman coolly swapped
off quite a number of votes for President
in consideration of votes given to their candidate for the State Legislature; and in 1885,
in my own district, a local Republican club
that had a member running for alderman,
performed a precisely similar feat in relation
to their party's candidate for governor. A
Tammany State Senator openly announced
in a public speech that it was of vastly more

importance to Tammany to have one of her own men Mayor of New York than it was to have a Democratic President of the United States. Very many of the leaders of the rival organizations, who lack the boldness to make such a frankly cynical avowal of what their party feeling really amounts to, yet in practice, both as regards mayor and as regards all other local offices which are politically or pecuniarily of importance, act exactly on the theory enunciated by the Tammany statesman; and, as a consequence, in every great election not only is it necessary to have the mass of the voters waked up to the importance of the principles that are at stake, but, unfortunately, it is also necessary to see that the powerful local leaders are convinced that it will be to their own interest to be faithful to the party ticket. Often there will be intense rivalry between two associations or two minor bosses; and one may take up and the other oppose the cause of a candidate with an earnestness and hearty good-will arising

by no means from any feeling for the man
himself, but from the desire to score a triumph over the opposition. It not unfre-
quently happens that a perfectly good man,
who would not knowingly suffer the least
impropriety in the conduct of his canvass,
is supported in some one district by a little
knot of politicians of shady character, who
have nothing in common with him at all, but
who wish to beat a rival body that is opposing him, and who do not for a moment hesi-
tate to use every device, from bribery down,
to accomplish their ends. A curious incident of this sort came to my knowledge
while happening to inquire how a certain
man became a Republican. It occurred a
good many years ago, and thanks to our
election laws it could not now be repeated
in all its details; but affairs similar in kind
occur at every election. I may preface it
by stating that the man referred to, whom
we will call X, ended by pushing himself
up in the world, thanks to his own industry
and integrity, and is now a well-to-do pri-

vate citizen and as good a fellow as anyone
would wish to see. But at the time spoken
of he was a young laborer, of Irish birth,
working for his livelihood on the docks and
associating with his Irish and American fellows. The district where he lived was over-
whelmingly Democratic, and the contests
were generally merely factional. One small
politician, a saloon-keeper named Larry, who
had a great deal of influence, used to enlist
on election day, by pay and other compensa-
tion, the services of the gang of young fellows to which X belonged. On one occasion he failed to reward them for their work,
and in other ways treated them so shabbily
as to make them very angry, more especially
X, who was their leader. There was no
way to pay Larry off until the next election;
but they determined to break his influence
utterly then, and as the best method for
doing this they decided to "vote as far away
from him" as possible, or, in other words,
to strain every nerve to secure the election
of all the candidates most opposed to those

whom Larry favored. After due consulta-
tion, it was thought that this could be most
surely done by supporting the Republican
ticket. Most of the other bodies of young
laborers, or, indeed, of young roughs, made
common cause with X and his friends. Everything was kept very quiet until election day,
neither Larry nor the few Republicans having an inkling of what was going on. It
was a rough district, and usually the Republican booths were broken up and their ballot-
distributers driven off early in the day; but
on this occasion, to the speechless astonish-
ment of everybody, things went just the
other way. The Republican ballots were
distributed most actively, the opposing
workers were bribed, persuaded, or frightened away, all means fair and foul were
tried and finally there was almost a riot,—
the outcome being that the Republicans actually obtained a majority in a district where
they had never before polled ten per cent.
of the total vote. Such a phenomenon attracted the attention of the big Republican

leaders, who after some inquiry found it was
due to X. To show their gratitude and to
secure so useful an ally permanently (for
this was before the days of civil-service reform), they procured him a lucrative place
in the New York Post-office; and he, in turn,
being a man of natural parts, at once seized
the opportunity, set to work to correct the
defects of his early education, and is now
what I have described him to be.

BOSS METHODS.

A POLITICIAN who becomes an influential
local leader or boss is, of course, always one
with a genuine talent for intrigue and organization. He owes much of his power to
the rewards he is able to dispense. Not only
does he procure for his supporters positions
in the service of the State or city,—as in
the custom-house, sheriff's office, etc.,—but
he is also able to procure positions for many
on horse railroads, the elevated roads, quarry
works, etc. Great corporations are peculiarly subject to the attacks of demagogues,

and they find it much to their interest to be
on good terms with the leader in each district who controls the vote of the Assemblyman and Alderman; and therefore the
former is pretty sure that a letter of rec-
ommendation from him on behalf of any
applicant for work will receive most favor-
able consideration. The leader is also continually helping his henchmen out of dif-
ficulties, pecuniary and otherwise; he lends
them a dollar or two now and then,
helps out, when possible, such of their
kinsmen as get into the clutches of the law,
gets a hold over such of them as have done
wrong and are afraid of being exposed, and
learns to mix judicious bullying with the
rendering of service.

But, in addition to all this, the boss owes
very much of his commanding influence to
his social relations with various bodies of his
constituents; and it is his work as well as his
pleasure to keep up these relations. No
débutante during her first winter in society
has a more exacting round of social duties

to perform than has a prominent ward politician. In every ward there are numerous
organizations, primarily social in character,
but capable of being turned to good account
politically. The Amalgamated Hack-driver's
Union, the Hibernian Republican Club, the
West Side Young Democrats, the Jefferson C.
Mullin Picnic Association,—there are twenty
such bodies as these in every district, and
with, at any rate, the master spirits in each
and all it is necessary for the boss to keep
on terms of intimate and, indeed, rather bois-
terous friendship. When the Jefferson C.
Mullin society goes on a picnic, the average
citizen scrupulously avoids its neighborhood ;
but the boss goes, perhaps with his wife, and,
moreover, enjoys himself heartily, and is
hail-fellow-well-met with the rest of the pic-
nickers, who, by the way, may be by no
means bad fellows; and when election day
comes round, the latter, in return, no matter
to what party they may nominally belong,
enthusiastically support their friend and
guest, on social, not political, grounds. The

boss knows every man in his district who can control any number of votes: an influential saloon-keeper, the owner of a large livery stable, the leader among a set of horse-car drivers, a foreman in a machine-shop who has a taste for politics,—with all alike he keeps up constant and friendly relations. Of course this fact does not of itself make the boss a bad man; there are several such I could point out who are ten times over better fellows than are the mild-mannered scholars of timorous virtue who criticise them. But on the whole the qualities tending to make a man a successful local political leader under our present conditions are not apt to be qualities that make him serve the public honestly or disinterestedly; and in the lower wards, where there is a large vicious population, the condition of politics is often fairly appalling, and the boss of the dominant party is generally a man of grossly immoral public and private character, as anyone can satisfy himself by examining the testimony taken by the last two or three legislative committees that have investigated the affairs of New York city. In some of these wards many of the social organizations with which the leaders are obliged to keep on good terms are composed of criminals, or of the relatives and associates of criminals. The testimony mentioned above showed some strange things. I will take at random a few instances that occur to me at the moment. There was one case of an assemblyman who served several terms in the Legislature, while his private business was to carry on corrupt negotiations between the Excise Commissioners and owners of low haunts who wished licenses. The president of a powerful semi-political association was by profession a burglar, the man who received the goods he stole was an alderman. Another alderman was elected while his hair was still short from a term in State Prison. A school trustee had been convicted of embezzlement, and was the associate of criminals. A prominent official in the Police Department was interested in dis-

reputable houses and gambling saloons, and
was backed politically by their proprietors.

BEATING THE MACHINE.

In the better wards the difficulty comes in
drilling a little sense and energy into decent
people: they either do not care to combine
or else refuse to learn how. In one district
we did at one time and for a considerable
period get control of affairs and elect a set
of almost ideal delegates and candidates to
the various nominating and legislative
bodies, and in the end took an absolutely
commanding although temporary position in
State and even in national politics.

This was done by the efforts of some
twenty or thirty young fellows who devoted a
large part of their time to thoroughly organizing and getting out the respectable vote.
The moving spirits were all active, energetic
men, with common sense, whose motives
were perfectly disinterested. Some went in
from principle; others, doubtless, from good-
fellowship or sheer love of the excitement

always attendant upon a political struggle. Our success was due to our absolute freedom from caste spirit. Among our chief workers were a Columbia College professor, a crack oarsman from the same institution, an Irish quarryman, a master carpenter, a rich young merchant, the owner of a small cigar store, the editor of a little German newspaper, and a couple of employees from the post-office and custom-house, who worked directly against their own seeming interests. One of our important committees was composed of a prominent member of a Jewish synagogue, of the son of a noted Presbyterian clergyman, and of a young Catholic lawyer. We won some quite remarkable tiiumphs, for the first time in New York politics carrying primaries against the machine, and as the result of our most successful struggle completely revolutionizing the State Convention held to send delegates to the National Republican Convention of 1884, and returning to that body, for the first and only time it was ever done a solid

delegation of Independent Republicans. This
was done, however, by sheer hard work on
the part of a score or so of men; the mass of
our good citizens, even after the victories
which they had assisted in winning, understood nothing about how they were won.
Many of them actually objected to organizing, apparently having a confused idea that
we could always win by what one of their
number called a " spontaneous uprising,"
to which a quiet young fellow in our camp
grimly responded that he had done a good
deal of political work in his day, but that he
never in his life had worked so hard and so
long as he did to get up the " spontaneous "
movement in which we were then engaged.

CONCLUSIONS.

In conclusion, it may be accepted as a
fact, however unpleasant, that if steady work
and much attention to detail are required,
ordinary citizens, to whom participation in
politics is merely a disagreeable duty, will
always be beaten by the organized army of

politicians to whom it is both duty, business, and pleasure, and who are knit together and to outsiders by their socal relations. On the other hand, average citizens do take a spasmodic interest in public affairs; and we should therefore so shape our governmental system that the action required by the voters should be as simple and direct as possible, and should not need to be taken any more often than is necessary. Governmental power should be concentrated in the hands of a very few men, who would be so conspicuous that no citizen could help knowing all about them; and the elections should not come too frequently. Not one decent voter in ten will take the trouble annually to inform himself as to the character of the host of petty candidates to be balloted for, but he will be sure to know all about the mayor, comptroller, etc. It is not to his credit that we can only rely, and that without much certainty, upon his taking a spasmodic interest in the government that affects his own well being; but such is the case, and accordingly we ought,

as far as possible, to have a system requir
ing on his part intermittent and not sus
tained action.

VII

THE VICE-PRESIDENCY AND THE CAMPAIGN OF 1896[1]

THE Vice-President is an officer unique in his character and functions, or to speak more properly, in his want of functions while he remains Vice-President, and in his possibility of at any moment ceasing to be a functionless official and becoming the head of the whole nation. There is no corresponding position in any constitutional government. Perhaps the nearest analogue is the heir apparent in a monarchy. Neither the French President nor the British Prime Minister has a substitute, ready at any moment to take his place, but exercising scarcely any authority until his place is

[1] *Review of Reviews*, September, 1896.

taken. The history of such an office is interesting, and the personality of the incumbent
for the time being may at any moment become of vast importance.

The founders of our government—the
men who did far more than draw up the
Declaration of Independence, for they put
forth the National Constitution—in many
respects builded very wisely of set purpose.
In some cases they built wiser than they
knew. In yet other instances they failed entirely to achieve objects for which they had
endeavored to provide by a most elaborate
and ingenious governmental arrangement.
They distrusted what would now be called
pure Democracy, and they dreaded what we
would now call party government.

Their distrust of Democracy induced them
to construct the electoral college for the
choice of a President, the original idea being that the people should elect their best
and wisest men who in turn should, untram-
meled by outside pressure, elect a President.
As a matter of fact the functions of the

electorate have now by time and custom become of little more importance than those of
so many letter-carriers. They deliver the
electoral votes of their states just as a let-
ter-carrier delivers his mail. But in the presidential contest this year it may be we shall
see a partial return to the ideals of the
men of 1789; for some of the electors on
the Bryan-Sewall-Watson ticket may exercise a choice between the vice-presidential
candidates.

The distrust felt by the founders of the
constitution for party government took shape
in. the scheme to provide that the majority
party should have the foremost place, and
the minority party the second place, in the
national executive. The man who received
the greatest number of electoral votes was
made President, and the man who received
the second greatest number was made Vice-
President, on a theory somewhat akin to that
by which certain reformers hope to revolu-
tionize our system of voting at the present
day. In the early days under the present

constitution this system resulted in the choice of Adams for President and of his anti-type Jefferson as Vice-President, the combination being about as incongruous as if we should now see McKinley President and either Bryan or Watson Vice-President. Even in theory such an arrangement is very bad, because under it the Vice-President might readily be, and as a matter of fact was, a man utterly opposed to all the principles to which the President was devoted, so that the arrangement provided in the event of the death of the President, not for a succession, but for a revolution. The system was very soon diopped, and each party nominated its own candidates for both positions. But it was many years before all the members of the electoral college of one party felt obliged to cast the same votes for both President and Vice-President, and consequently there was a good deal of scrambling and shifting in taking the vote. When, however, the parties had crystallized into Democratic and Whig, a score of years after the disappearance of the Federalists, the system of party voting also crystallized. Each party then as a rule nominated one man for President and one for Vice-President, these being voted for throughout the nation. This system in turn speedily produced strange results, some of which remain to this day. There are and must be in every party factions. The victorious faction may crush out and destroy the others, or it may try to propitiate at least its most formidable rival. In consequence, the custom grew of offering the vice-presidency as a consolation prize, to be given in many cases to the very men who were most bitterly opposed to the nomination of the successful candidate for President. Sometimes this consolation prize was awarded for geographical reasons, sometimes to bring into the party men who on points of principle might split away because of the principles of the presidential candidate himself, and at other times it was awarded for merely factional reasons to some faction which did not differ in the least from the dominant faction in matters of principles, but had very decided views on the question of offices.

The presidency being all important, and the vice-presidency of comparatively little note, the entire strength of the contending factions is spent in the conflict over the first, and very often a man who is most anxious to take the first place will not take the second, preferring some other political position. It has thus frequently happened that the two candidates have been totally dissimilar in character and even in party principle, though both running on the same ticket. Very odd results have followed in more than one instance.

A striking illustration of the evils sometimes springing from this system is afforded by what befell the Whigs after the election and death of the elder Harrison. Translated into the terms of the politics of continental Europe of to-day, Harrison's adherents represented a union between the right and the extreme left against the centre. That is, the

regular Whigs who formed the bulk of his
supporters were supplemented by a small
body of extremists who in their political principles were even more alien to the Whigs
than were the bulk of the regular Democrats, but who themselves hated these regular Democrats with the peculiar ferocity so
often felt by the extremist for the man who
goes far, but not quite far enough. In consequence, the President represented Whig
principles, the Vice-President represented a
rather extreme form of the very principles
to which the Whigs were most opposed. The
result was that when Harrison died the presidency fell into the hands of a man who had
but a corporal's guard of supporters in the
nation, and who proceeded to oppose all the
measures of the immense majority of those
who elected him.

A somewhat similar instance was afforded
in the case of Lincoln and Johnson. Johnson was put on the ticket largely for geographical reasons, and on the death of Lincoln he tried to reverse the policy of the

party which had put him in office. An instance of an entirely different kind is afforded
by Garfield and Arthur. The differences between these two party leaders were mainly
merely factional. Each stood squarely on
the platform of the party, and all the principles advocated by one were advocated by
the other; yet the death of Garfield meant a
complete overturn in the *personnel* of the upper Republican officials, because Arthur had
been nominated expressly to placate the
group of party leaders who most objected to
the nomination of Garfield. Arthur made
a very good President, but the bitterness
caused by his succession to power nearly tore
the party in twain. It will be noted that
most of these evils arose from the fact that
the Vice-President under ordinary circumstances possesses so little real power. He presides over the Senate and he has in Washington a position of marked social importance, but his political weight as Vice-
President is almost *nil*. There is always a
chance that he may become President. As

this is only a chance it seems quite impossible to persuade politicians to give it proper weight. This certainly does not seem right. The Vice-President should, so far as possible, represent the same views and principles which have secured the nomination and election of the President, and he should be a man standing well in the councils of the party, trusted by his fellow party leaders, and able in the event of any accident to his chief to take up the work of the latter just where it was left. The Republican party has this year nominated such a man in the person of Mr. Hobart. But nominations of this kind have by no means always been the rule of recent years. No change of parties, for instance, could well produce a greater revolution in policy than would have been produced at almost any time during the last three years if Mr. Cleveland had died and Mr. Stevenson had succeeded him.

One sure way to secure this desired result would undoubtedly be to increase the power of the Vice-President. He should always be a man who would be consulted by the President on every great party question. It would be very well if he were given a seat in the Cabinet. It might be well if, in addition to his vote in the Senate in the event of a tie, he should be given a vote, on ordinary occasions, and perchance on occasions a voice in the debates. A man of the character of Mr. Hobart is sure to make his weight felt in an administration, but the power of thus exercising influence should be made official rather than personal.

The present contest offers a striking illustration of the way in which the Vice-President ought and ought not to be nominated, and to study this it is necessary to study not only the way in which the different candidates were nominated, but at least in outline the characters of the candidates themselves.

For the first time in many years, indeed for the first time since parties have fairly crystallized along their present lines, there are three parties running, two of which support the same presidential candidate but dif-

ferent candidates for the vice-presidency.
Each one of these parties has carried several states during the last three or four years.
Each party has a right to count upon a number of electoral votes as its own. Closely though the Democratic and Populistic parties have now approximated in their principles as enunciated in the platforms of Chicago and St. Louis, they yet do differ on certain points, and neither would have any chance of beating the Republicans without the help of the other. The result has been a coalition, yet each party to the coalition has retained enough of its jealous individuality to make it refuse to accept the candidate of the other for the second position on the ticket.

The Republican party stands on a normal and healthy party footing. It has enunciated a definite set of principles entirely in accord with its past actions. It has nominated on this platform a President and Vice-President, both of whom are thorough-going believers in all the party principles set forth in

the platform upon which they stand. Mr.
McKinley believes in sound finance,—that
is, in a currency based upon gold and as
good as gold. So does Mr. Hobart. Mr.
McKinley believes in a protective tariff. So
does Mr. Hobart. Mr. McKinley believes in
the only method of preserving orderly liberty,
—that is, in seeing that the laws are en-
forced at whatever cost. So does Mr. Hobart. In short Mr. Hobart stands for precisely the same principles that are represented by Mr. McKinley. He is a man of
weight in the community, who has had wide
experience both in business and in politics.
He is taking an active part in the campaign,
and he will be a power if elected to the
vice-presidency. All the elements which have
rallied behind Mr. McKinley are just as
heartily behind Mr. Hobart. The two represent the same forces, and they stand for a
party with a coherent organization and a
definite purpose, to the carrying out of which
they are equally pledged.

It will be a matter of much importance to

the nation that the next Vice-President should stand for some settled policy. It is an unhealthy thing to have the Vice-President and President represented by principles so far apart that the succession of one to the place of the other means a change as radical as any possible party overturn. The straining and dislocation of our governmental institutions was very great when Tyler succeeded Harrison and Johnson succeeded Lincoln. In each case the majority of the party that had won the victory felt that it had been treated with scandalous treachery, for Tyler grew to be as repulsive to the Whigs as Polk himself, and the Republicans could scarcely have hated Seymour more than they hated Johnson. The Vice-President has a three-fold relation. First to the administration; next as presiding officer in the Senate, where he should be a man of dignity and force; and third in his social position, for socially he ranks second to the President alone. Mr. Morton was in every way an admirable Vice-President under

General Harrison, and had he succeeded to the presidential chair there would have been no break in the great policies which were being pushed forward by the administration. But during Mr. Cleveland's two incumbencies Messrs. Hendricks and Stevenson have represented, not merely hostile factions, but principles and interests from which he was sundered by a gulf quite as great as that which divided him from his normal party foes. Mr. Sewall would make a colorless Vice-President, and were he at any time to succeed Mr. Bryan in the White House would travel Mr. Bryan's path only with extreme reluctance and under duress. Mr. Watson would be a more startling, more attractive, and more dangerous figure, for if he got the chance he would lash the nation with a whip of scorpions, while Mr. Bryan would be content with the torture of ordinary thongs.

Finally, Mr. Hobart would typify as strongly as Mr. McKinley himself what was best in the Republican party and in the nation, and would stand as one of the known champions of his party on the very questions at issue in the present election. He is a man whose advice would be sought by all who are prominent in the administration. In short, he would be the kind of man whom the electors are certain to choose as Vice-President if they exercise their choice rationally.

The men who left the Republican party because of the nomination of McKinley would have left it just as quickly if Hobart had been nominated. They do not believe in sound finance, and though many of the bolters object to anarchy and favor protection, they feel that in this crisis their personal desires must be repressed and that they are conscientiously bound to support the depreciated dollar even at the cost of incidentally supporting the principles of a low tariff and the doctrine that a mob should be allowed to do what it likes with immunity. There are many advocates of clipped or depreciated money who are rather sorry to see the demand for such currency coupled with a de-

mand for more lawlessness and an abandon-
ment by the government of the police functions which are the essential attributes of
civilization; but they have overcome their
reluctance, feeling that on the whole it is
more important that the money of the nation should be unsound than that its laws
should be obeyed. People who feel this way
are just as much opposed to Mr. Hobart as
to Mr. McKinley. They object to the platform upon which the two men stand, and
they object as much to the character of one
man as to the character of the other. They
are repelled by McKinley's allegiance to the
cause of sound money, and find nothing to
propitiate them in Hobart's uncompromis-
ingly honest attitude on the same question.
There is no reason whatever why any voter
who would wish to vote against the one
should favor the other, or *vice versa*.

When we cross the political line all this is
changed. On the leading issue of the campaign the entire triangle of candidates are a
unit. Mr. Bryan, the nominee for the presi-

dency, and Messrs. Sewall and Watson, the
nominees for the vice-presidency, are almost
equally devoted adherents of the light-weight
dollar and of a currency which shall not force
a man to repay what he has borrowed, and
shall punish the wrong-headed laborer, who
expects to be paid his wages in money worth
something, as heavily as the business man or
farmer who is so immoral as to wish to pay
his debts. All three are believers in that old-
world school of finance which appears under
such protean changes of policy, always de-
siring the increase of the circulating medium,
but differing as to the means, which in one
age takes the form of putting base metal in
with the good, or of clipping the good, and
in another assumes the guise of fiat money,
or the free coinage of silver. On this currency question they are substantially alike,
agreeing (as one of their adherents pictur-
esquely put it, in arguing in favor of that
form of abundant currency which has as
its highest exponent the money of the late
Confederacy) that " the money which was

good enough for the soldiers of Washington
is good enough for us." As a matter of fact
the soldiers of Washington were not at all
grateful for the money which the loud-
mouthed predecessors of Mr. Bryan and his
kind then thought " good enough " for them.
The money with which the veterans of Washington were paid was worth two cents on the
dollar, and as yet neither Mr. Bryan, Mr.
Sewall, nor Mr. Watson has advocated a two-
cent copper dollar. Still, they are striving
toward this ideal, and in their advocacy of the
fifty cent dollar they are one.

But beyond this they begin to differ. Mr.
Sewall distinctly sags behind the leader of
the spike team, Mr. Bryan, and still more
distinctly behind his rival, or running mate,
or whatever one may choose to call him, the
Hon. Thomas Watson. There is far more
regard for the essential fitness of things in
a ticket which contains Mr. Bryan and Mr.
Watson than one which contains Mr. Bryan
and Mr. Sewall. Mr. Watson is a man of
Mr. Bryan's type, only a little more so. But

Mr. Sewall is of a different type, and possesses many attributes which must make association with him exceedingly painful, not merely to Mr. Watson, but to Mr. Bryan himself. He is a well-to-do man. Indeed in many communities he would be called a rich man. He is a banker, a railroad man, a shipbuilder, and has been successful in business. Now if Mr. Bryan and Mr. Watson really stand for any principle it is hostility to this kind of success. Thrift, industry, and business energy are qualities which are quite incompatible with true Populistic feeling. Payment of debts, like the suppression of riots, is abhorrent to the Populistic mind. Such conduct strikes the Populist as immoral. Mr. Bryan made his appearance in Congress with two colleagues elected on the same ticket, one of whom stated to the present writer that no honest man ever earned $5000 a year; that whoever got that amount stole it. Mr. Sewall has earned many times $5000 a year. He is a prosperous capitalist. Populism never prospers save where men are unprosperous, and your true Populist is especially intolerant of business success. If a man is a successful business man he at once calls him a plutocrat.

He makes only one exception. A miner or speculator in mines may be many times a millionaire and yet remain in good standing in the Populist party. The Populist has ineradicably fixed in his mind the belief that silver is a cheap metal, and that silver money is, while not fiat money, still a long step toward it. Silver is connected in his mind with scaling down debts, the partial repudiation of obligations, and other measures aimed at those odious moneyed tyrants who lend money to persons who insist upon borrowing, or who have put their ill-gotten gains in saving banks and kindred wicked institutions for the encouragement of the vice of thrift. These pleasurable associations quite outweigh, with the Populist, the fact that the silver man himself is rich. He is even for the moment blind to the further fact that these pro-silver men, like Senator Stewart,

Governor Altgeld, and their compeers, strenuously insist that the obligations to themselves shall be liquidated in gold; indeed this
particular idiosyncrasy of the silver leaders
is not much frowned upon by the bulk of
the Populists, because it has at least the merit
of savoring strongly of " doing " one's creditors. Not even the fact that rich silver mine
owners may have earned their money honestly can outweigh the other fact that they
champion a species of currency which will
make most thrifty and honest men poorer, in
the minds of the truly logical Populist.

But Mr. Sewall has no fictitious advantage
in the way of owing his wealth to silver. He
has made his money precisely as the most
loathed reprobate of Wall Street—or of New
York, which the average Populist regards
as synonymous with Wall Street—has made
his. The average Populist does not draw
fine distinctions. There are in New York, as
in other large cities, scoundrels of great
wealth who have made their money by means
skilfully calculated to come just outside the

line of criminality. There are other men
who have made their money exactly as the
successful miner or farmer makes his,—that
is, by the exercise of shrewdness, business
daring, energy and thrift. But the Populist
draws no line of division between these two
classes. They have made money, and that is
enough. One may have built railroads and
the other have wrecked them, but they are
both railroad men in his eyes, and that is all.
One may have swindled his creditors, and
the other built up a bank which has been of
incalculable benefit to all who have had dealings with it, but to the Populist they are both
gold bugs, and as such noxious. Mr. Sewall
is the type of man the contemplation of which
usually throws a Populist orator into spasms.
But it happens that he believes in free silver, just as other very respectable men believe in spirit rapping, or the faith-cure, or
Buddhism, or pilgrimages to Lourdes, or the
foot of a graveyard rabbit. There are very
able men and very lovely women who believe
in each or all of these. and there are a much

larger number who believe in free silver.
Had they lived in the days of Sparta they
would have believed in free iron, iron coin
being at that time the cheapest circulating
medium, the adoption of which would give
the greatest expansion of the currency. But
they have been dragged on by the slow procession of the centuries, and now they only
believe in free silver. It is a belief which is
compatible with all the domestic virtues, and
even occasionally with very good capacities
as a public servant. Mr. Sewall doubtless
stands as one of these men. He can hardly
be happy, planted firmly as he is, on the Chicago platform. In the minds of most thrifty,
hard-working men, who are given to thinking at all about public questions, the free-
silver plank is very far from being the most
rotten of the many rotten planks put together
with such perverted skill by the Chicago
architects. A platform which declares in
favor of free and unlimited rioting and
which has the same strenuous objection to the
exercise of the police power by the general

government that is felt in the circles presided over by Herr Most, Eugene V. Debs, and all the people whose pictures appear in the detective bureaus of our great cities, cannot appeal to persons who have gone beyond the unpolished-stone period of civilization.

The men who object to what they style " government by injunction " are, as regards the essential principles of government, in hearty sympathy with their remote skin-clad ancestors who lived in caves, fought one another with stone-headed axes, and ate the mammoth and woolly rhinoceros. They are interesting as representing a geological survival, but they are dangerous whenever there is the least chance of their making the principles of this ages-buried past living factors in our present life. They are not in sympathy with men of good minds and sound civic morality. It is not a nice thing to wish to pay one's debts in coins worth fifty cents on the dollar, but it is a much less nice thing to wish to plunge one's country into anarchy by providing that the law shall only protect the lawless and frown scornfully on the law-abiding. There is a good deal of mushy sentiment in the world, and there are always a certain number of people whose minds are weak and whose emotions are strong and who effervesce with sympathy toward any man who does wrong, and with indignation against any man who chastises the criminal for having done wrong. These emotionalists, moreover, are always reinforced by that large body of men who themselves wish to do wrong, and who are not sentimental at all, but, on the contrary, very practical. It is rarely that these two classes control a great political party, but at Chicago this became an accomplished fact.

Furthermore, the Chicago convention attacked the Supreme Court. Again this represents a species of atavism,—that is, of recurrence to the ways of thought of remote barbarian ancestors. Savages do not like an independent and upright judiciary. They want the judge to decide their way, and if he does not, they want to behead him. The

Populists experience much the same emotions when they realize that the judiciary stands between them and plunder.

Now on all these points Mr. Sewall can hardly feel complete sympathy with his temporary allies. He is very anxious that the Populists shall vote for him for Vice-President, and of course he feels a kindly emotion toward those who do intend to vote for him. He would doubtless pardon much heresy of political belief in any member of the electoral college who feels that Sewall is his friend, not Watson,—Codlin, not Short. He has, of course, a vein of the erratic in his character, or otherwise he would not be in such company at all, and would have no quality that would recommend him to them. But on the whole his sympathies must lie with the man who saves money rather than with the man who proposes to take away the money when it has been saved, and with the policeman who arrests a violent criminal rather than with the criminal. Such sympathy puts him at a disadvantage in the Populist camp. He is loud in his professions of belief in the remarkable series of principles for which he is supposed to stand, but his protestations ring rather hollow. The average supporter of Bryan doubtless intends to support Sewall, for he thinks him an unimportant tail to the Bryan kite. But, though unimportant, he regards him with a slight feeling of irritation, as being at the best a rather ludicrous contrast to the rest of the kite. He contributes no element of strength to the Bryan ticket, for other men who work hard and wish to enjoy the fruits of their toil simply regard him as a renegade, and the average Populist, or Populistic Democrat, does not like him, and accepts him simply because he fears not doing so may jeopardize Bryan's chances. He is in the uncomfortable position always held by the respectable theorist who gets caught in a revolutionary movement and has to wedge nervously up into the front rank with the gentlemen who are not troubled by any of his scruples, and who really do think that

it is all very fine and glorious. In fact Mr.
Sewall is much the least picturesque and the
least appropriate figure on the platform or
platforms upon which Mr. Bryan is standing.

Mr. Watson, whose enemies now call him
a Georgia cracker, is in reality a far more
suitable companion for Mr. Bryan in such
a contest. It must be said, however, that
if virtue always received its reward Mr. Watson and not Mr. Bryan would stand at the
head of the ticket. In the language of mathe-
maticians Mr. Watson merely represents Mr.
Bryan raised several powers. The same is
true of the Populist as compared to the
Democratic platform. Mr. Bryan may affect to believe that free silver does represent
the ultimate goal, and that his friends do not
intend to go further in the direction of fiat
money. Mr. Watson's friends, the middle-
of-the-road Populists, are much more fearless and much more logical. They are willing to accept silver as a temporary makeshift,
but they want a currency based on corn and

cotton next, and ultimately a currency based on the desires of the people who issue it. The statesmanlike utterance of that great financier, Mr. Bryan's chief rival for the nomination and at present his foremost supporter, Mr. Bland, to the effect that he would "wipe out the national debt as with a sponge," meets with their cordial approval as far as it goes, but they object to the qualification before the word "debt." In wiping out debts they do not wish to halt merely at the national debt. The Populists indorsed Bryan as the best they could get; but they hated Sewall so that they took the extraordinary step of nominating the Vice-President before the President so as to make sure of a really acceptable man in the person of Watson.

With Mr. Bryan denunciation of the gold bug and the banker is largely a mere form of intellectual entertainment; but with Mr. Watson it represents an almost ferocious conviction. Someone has said that Mr. Watson like Mr. Tillman, is an embodied retribution on the South for having failed to educate the cracker, the poor white who gives him his strength. It would ill beseem any dweller in cities of the North, especially any dweller in the city of Tammany, to reproach the South with having failed to educate anybody. But Mr. Watson is certainly an awkward man for a community to develop. He is infinitely more in earnest than is Mr. Bryan. Mr. Watson's followers belong to that school of southern Populists who honestly believe that the respectable and commonplace people who own banks, railroads, dry-goods stores, factories, and the like, are persons with many of the mental and social attributes that unpleasantly distinguished Heliogabalus, Nero, Caligula, and other worthies of later Rome. Not only do they believe this, but they say it with appalling frankness. They are very sincere as a rule, or at least the rank and file are. They are also very suspicious. They distrust anything they cannot understand; and as they understand but little this opens a very wide

field for distrust. They are apt to be emo-
tionally religious. If not, they are then at
least atheists of an archaic type. Refinement
and comfort they are apt to consider quite
as objectionable as immorality. That a man
should change his clothes in the evening,
that he should dine at any other hour than
noon, impress these good people as being
symptoms of depravity instead of merely tri-
vial. A taste for learning and cultivated
friends, and a tendency to bathe frequently,
cause them the deepest suspicion. A well-
to-do man they regard with jealous distrust,
and if they cannot be well-to-do themselves,
at least they hope to make matters uncomfortable for those that are. They possess
many strong, rugged virtues, but they are
quite impossible politically, because they always confound the essentials and the non-
essentials, and though they often make war
on vice, they rather prefer making war upon
prosperity and refinement.

Mr. Watson was in a sense born out of
place when he was born in Georgia, for in

Georgia the regular Democracy, while it has accepted the principles of the Populists, has made war on their *personnel,* and in every way strives to press them down. Far better for Mr. Watson would it have been could he have been born in the adjacent State of South Carolina, where the Populists swallowed the Democrats with a gulp. Senator Tillman, the great Populist or Democratic orator from South Carolina, possesses an untrammelled tongue any middle-of-the-road man would envy: and moreover Mr. Tillman's brother has been frequently elected to Congress upon the issue that he never wore either an overcoat or an undershirt, an issue which any Populist statesman finds readily comprehensible, and which he would recognize at first glance as being strong before the people. It needs a certain amount of mental subtlety to appreciate that it is for one's interest to support a man because he is honest and has broad views about coast defenses and the navy, and other similar subjects; but it does not need any mind at all to

haye one's prejudices stirred in favor of a
statesman whose claim to the title deststupon
his indifference to the requirements of civilized dress.

Altogether Mr. Watson, with his sincerity;
his frankness, his extreme suspiciousness, his
distrust of anything he cannot understand,
and the feeling he encourages against all the
elegancies and decencies of civilized life, is
an interesting personage. He represents the
real thing while Bryan after all is more or
less a sham and a compromise. Mr Watson would, at a blow destroy all banks and
bankers with a cheerful, albeit vague, belief that thereby he was in some abstruse way
benefiting the people at large. And he
would do this with the simple sincerity and
faith of an African savage who tries to benefit his tribe by a sufficiency of human sacri-
fices. But Mr. Bryan would be beset by ugly
doubts when he came to put into effect all the
mischievous beliefs of his followers, and Mr.
Sewall would doubtless be frankly miserable
if it ever became necessary for him to take

a lead in such matters. Mr. Watson really ought to be the first man on the ticket, with Mr. Bryan second; for he is much the superior in boldness, in thorough-going acceptance of his principles according to their logical conclusions, and in sincerity of faith. It is impossible not to regret that the Democrats and Populists should not have put forward in the first place the man who genuinely represents their ideas.

However, it is even doubtful whether Mr. Watson will receive the support to which he is entitled as a vice-presidential candidate. In the South the Populists have been so crushed under the heel of the Democrats, and have bitten that heel with such eager venom, that they dislike entering into a coalition with them; but in the south the Democrats will generally control the election machinery. In the far West, and generally in those States where the Populist wing of the new alliance is ascendant, the Populists have no especial hatred of the Democrats. They know that their principles are substantially identical, and they think it best to support the man who seems to represent the majority faction among the various factions that stand behind Bryan.

As a consequence of this curious condition of affairs there are several interesting possibilities open. The electoral college consists of the men elected at the polls in the various States to record the decrees of the majorities in those States, and it has grown to be an axiom of politics that they must merely register the will of the men who elected them. But it does seem possible that in the present election some of the electors may return to the old principles of a century ago and exercise at least a limited discretion in casting their votes. In a State like Nebraska, for instance, it looks as though it would be possible that the electoral ticket on the anti-Republican side would be composed of four Bryan and Watson men and four Bryan and Sewall men. Now in the event of Bryan having more votes than McKinley—that is, in the event of the country

showing strong Bedlamite tendencies next
November—it might be that a split between
Sewall and Watson would give a plurality to
Hobart, and in such event it is hardly conceivable that some of the electors would not
exercise their discretion by changing their
votes. If they did not, we might then again
see a return to the early and profoundly interesting practice of our fathers and witness
a President chosen by one party and a Vice-
President by the other.

I wish it to be distinctly understood, however, that these are merely interesting specu-
lations as to what might occur in a hopelessly
improbable contingency. I am a good American, with a profound belief in my country-
meh, and I have no idea that they will deliberately lower themselves to a level beneath
that of a South American Republic, by voting for the farrago of sinister nonsense
which the Populistic-Democratic politicians
at Chicago chose to set up as embodying the
principles of their party, and for the amiable
and windy demagogue who stands upon that

platform. Many entirely honest and intelligent men have been misled by the silver talk, and have for the moment joined the ranks of the ignorant, the vicious and the wrong-headed. These men of character and capacity are blinded by their own misfortunes, or their own needs, or else they have never fairly looked into the matter for themselves, being, like most men, whether in " gold " or " silver " communities, content to follow the opinion of those they are accustomed to trust. After full and fair inquiry these men, I am sure, whether they live in Maine, in Tennessee, or in Oregon, will come out on the side of honest money. The shiftless and vicious and the honest but hopelessly ignorant and puzzle-headed voters cannot be reached; but the average farmer, the average business man, the average workman—in short, the average American—will always stand up for honesty and decency when he can once satisfy himself as to the side on which they are to be found.

9 781589 633216